Introdu

The **northern part** of the Snowdo[...] Wales, is a stunningly diverse lands[...] lakes and wooded valleys formed dur[...] [...] derives from Snowdon (Yr Wyddfa), the highest mo[...] [...]and and Wales. Whilst attracting millions of visitors each year [...]ains a living landscape which has been shaped by traditional hill farming, quarrying for slate as well as mining for lead and copper. Northern Snowdonia is an area steeped in Welsh history, language and culture, while offering a tremendous variety of walking opportunities.

In this book I have selected 30 walks, some in less well known areas, which reflect northern Snowdonia's rich diversity of landscape, scenic value and historic interest. There are walks exploring the coastal foothills of the Carneddau range from above Conwy to Bethesda, including the stunning Aber Falls and a climb up Tal y Fan, Snowdonia's most northerly mountain. There are waymarked trails through Gwydyr Forest Park past hidden upland lakes and lead-mining relics. They visit ancient monuments including Iron Age hillforts, stone circles and standing stones, and a remote upland medieval church. They follow in the footsteps of Romans, drovers and miners and pass close to Snowdon Mountain and the Welsh Highland Narrow Gauge Steam Railways. There are walks by rivers, through woodland, past valley and upland lakes. They visit historic communities, including popular Betws-y-Coed, Beddgelert and Llanberis, as well as the former slate quarry village of Cwm Penmachno.

They range from a 1½ mile waymarked National Trust woodland and upland trail to a challenging 8 mile ridge walk, one of the best in Snowdonia. They follow public rights of way and permissive paths or cross Open Access land. A key feature is that many individual routes, as well as containing shorter walk options, can easily be linked with others, to provide longer day walks, if required.

Be properly prepared and equipped for this mountainous area, where weather conditions can quickly change. Walking boots are required, along with provisions, map and appropriate clothing to protect against the elements. Please remember that path conditions can vary according to season and weather, and that even low level paths can be rocky or muddy. Refer any public path problems encountered to Gwynedd Council Rights of Way section (www.gwynedd.gov.uk).

Each walk has a detailed map and description, but bear in mind that changes in detail can occur at any time. The location of each walk is shown on the back cover and a summary of their key features is also given. This includes an estimated walking time, but allow more time to enjoy the scenery and sights.

Please observe the country code. Enjoy your walking!

WALK 1
CONWY MOUNTAIN

DESCRIPTION A delightful 3¾ mile (**A**) or 3 mile (**B**) walk exploring Conwy Mountain, offering panoramic views. The outward route provides an optional additional ½ mile extension to visit a former quarry, before climbing onto its rocky ridge (800 feet/244 metres) containing an Iron Age fort. It then descends the superb ridge towards Conwy, before returning on the waymarked North Wales Path/Wales Coast Path across its southern slopes. Allow about 3 hours.
START Top of Sychnant Pass [SH 750770]
DIRECTIONS Follow the one way system west through Conwy past the railway station. After passing under the town walls, turn left up Mount Pleasant. At the T- junction turn right past the youth hostel and follow the road to the top of Sychnant Pass.

1 Take the signposted North Wales Path (NWP) down a rough lane passing beneath crags at the head of an impressive valley. It is joined by the Wales Coast Path (WCP) and rises, then continues as a stony track. Shortly it bends left to a finger post. Here turn RIGHT with the NWP through a nearby gate and up the stony track ahead, shortly descending to a crossroad of narrow tracks by a waymark post. Keep ahead with the NWP/WCP to reach another waymark post – *with a great view ahead over the quarried hillside to Llandudno and the Great Orme*. (For the quarry extension follow the path ahead down and across the bracken slope onto the wide grass shelf, then return to the waymark post.)

2 Bear RIGHT up the NWP/WCP, then at another post where the NWP/WCP bears right, keep ahead up the stony path, then at a crossroad of paths angle LEFT up the stony path to another path junction. Turn LEFT along the wide path, soon rising. When it splits go up the stonier left fork on to Conwy Mountain – *offering extensive coastal views*. Soon take the path's right fork up onto the small ridge ahead to pass through Caer Seion hillfort with its stone entrance visible below.

It was used between 2300–1900 years ago and contained about 50 round buildings. Shortly the ridge path makes a rocky descent. (An adjoining path on the left below the ridge is an easier option.) *There is a great view down to Conwy with its impressive late 13thC castle. It was built for Edward I to strengthen his conquest of Wales, along with a new town for English settlers, enclosed by walls over ¾ mile in length and originally with 22 towers. The main path then levels out – with a view down to Conwy and Deganwy marinas. Shortly it descends again beneath high ground and bends down to the end of a nearby south-facing large rock slab – with a good view along the Conwy Valley.* (For **Walk B** go to a NWP/WCP waymarker post just below to join the returning route at point 4.)

3 Take a wide path continuing east along the ridge, soon descending steadily. At a crossroad of paths either continue down the path or turn LEFT along a small ridge to a metal post overlooking the coast. *Nearby is the remains of a quarry which once produced millstone used for grinding flour.* Turn around and take a path angling LEFT down and across the slope, rising to rejoin the ridge path. Continue down the path, soon by a woodland boundary. At the wall corner the path bends down and round to a ladder-stile above a house, then descends to a road. Follow it RIGHT. Take the signposted NWP/

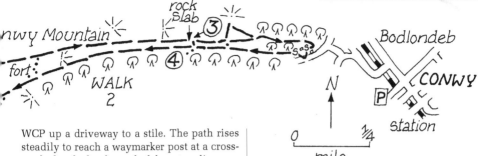

WCP up a driveway to a stile. The path rises steadily to reach a waymarker post at a crossroad of paths by the rock slab met earlier.

4 Follow the NWP/WCP beneath the rock slab then on a long steady climb across the southern slopes of Conwy Mountain – *enjoying a good view of Tal-y-fan and the Carneddau mountains* – later passing an information board on Caer Seion. Soon after a bench seat the path makes a short descent and splits at a waymark post. Here you leave the NWP/WCP by descending the left fork to join the stony track near the wall below. Follow it to your outward route at the crossroad of tracks. Keep ahead, then take the narrow green left fork up through gorse, then bend LEFT along a wider track down the gate on your outward route. At the stony access track beyond take the signposted NWP over the rise opposite and down to rejoin the track. Follow it back to the start.

WALK 2

ALLTWEN & PENMAEN-BACH

DESCRIPTION An enjoyable 2 mile walk exploring an attractive heather covered Open Access area adjoining Conwy Mountain, featuring two small hills, an Iron Age hillfort, and panoramic views. Allow about 1½ hours. It can easily be linked to Walk 1 to make a great 4¾ mile circuit.

START Top of Sychnant Pass [SH 750770] See **Walk 1.**

1 Take the signposted North Wales Path along a rough lane passing beneath crags and rising. At a waymark post opposite a wall corner take a stony path up the heath-er-covered slope of Alltwen to its summit for superb all-round mountain and coastal views. Follow a path down its northern side towards a lower top, soon angling RIGHT down to cross the heather-covered ramparts of the hillfort. The path now descends more steeply through heather then gorse to a crossroad of paths in a dip. Follow the path ahead and just beyond a small post take its left fork up to a small rise. Follow the path across the hillside, soon descending and continuing past a wall. Follow the path ahead towards Penmaen-bach – *enjoying extensive coastal views* – soon rising beneath a small crag to reach a wall corner. Take a path on the left up Penmaen-bach to a stone cairn on a ridge overlooking the coast. Retrace your steps then after about 15 yards take another path leading LEFT up over nearby high ground to the hill's small rocky top. Follow the path down to the wall corner – *enjoying a good view of the heavily quarried hillside ahead.* Go ahead alongside the wall then up the green track, soon levelling out then descending.

2 The track then bends right. (To link with Walk 1 angle left down a path to a crosspath below. Follow it left to join the North Wales Path at a nearby waymark post at point 2 of **Walk 1.**) Follow the track down to a crossroad of paths/tracks. Here follow the track RIGHT towards Alltwen, then take its left fork, over a cross-track, soon bending right and descending. Just before a gate by sheepfolds and the entrance to Pen Pyra turn LEFT to follow the fence to go through a gate at a track. Go to a finger post ahead, then follow the access track back to the start.

WALK 3
MAEN ESGOB

DESCRIPTION A 4 mile (**A**) or 2¾ mile (**B**) walk using the network of delightful paths and tracks to explore attractive upland country, featuring several low hills offering panoramic views. The route first climbs nearby Cogwrn then meanders into open country to visit the small top of Maen Esgob (984 feet/300 metres). Walk A continues across Waen Gyrach, before returning to join Walk B for a visit to the small crag of Craigyfedwen. Allow about 2½ hours.

START Snowdonia National Park Sychnant car park [SH 755769]

DIRECTIONS Follow the one way system west through Conwy past the railway station. After passing under the town walls, turn left up Mount Pleasant. At the T-junction turn right past the youth hostel. Continue along the road, past a road and car park on the left, and up past the entrance to Penysychnant Nature Conservation Centre to find the signposted car park along a lane on the left.

1 From the north eastern corner of the car park take a path up to the top of Cogwrn, then walk along its small ridge and down its southern slope to join the nearby stony track. Follow it up to a track junction, then take the left fork down to the entrance to a cottage. Continue down a path to join a road by Ty Coch farm. Go along the road then at the end of terraced cottages take a signposted path up a rough access lane on the right. On its bend keep ahead up a wide path to rejoin the lane. Go past Encil-y-coed, then turn LEFT across the access track to Llechan Uchaf and follow a path up by the wall past a small enclosed reservoir. Go up the stony track ahead, keeping to its right fork, soon alongside a wall. At its corner just below a large house keep ahead to follow a green track up the bracken covered hillside to join a cross-track near a wall corner.

2 Follow it LEFT then after a few yards take its right fork, soon passing a small shallow pool. Just beyond take a path on the left up the heather covered slopes of Maen

Esgob to a small stone cairn on its top. (For **Walk B** take the alternative path back down to the track and join the wall beyond, then follow instructions from paragraph **6** of **Walk 4**.) For **Walk A** follow a delightful path down its southern slopes, soon passing above a side valley containing the shallow lake of Llyn y Wrach. Take the second path on the right down to a crossroad of paths in a hollow. Keep ahead through gorse then follow a wide path angling RIGHT up the hillside and across the wide heather/gorse top of Waen Gyrach towards Tal-y-fan, later angling down to join a green track near a wall.

3 Here turn sharp LEFT and follow the track back to point **2** near the wall corner. Keep ahead down the track then on the bend take the path angling RIGHT, then another path leading RIGHT to the small rocky top of Craigyfedwen. Take a nearby path down to rejoin the track. Follow it down to join your outward route, then follow either the lakeside path or the track back to the start.

WALK 4
MAEN PENDDU

DESCRIPTION A 7¼ mile upland walk (**A**) which extends Walk 3A to visit several of the area's interesting features. After Waen Gyrach the route climbs onto Cefn Maen Amor to visit large erratic boulders (1286 feet/392 metres). After visiting Maen Penddu standing stone, the route returns by a delightful green track, visits nearby upland reservoirs (optional), then follows a section of the North Wales Path, before rejoining Walk 3 for a final view from Craigyfedwen. Allow about 5 hours. The route includes an alternative 5 mile walk (**B**).

START As **Walk 3**.

1-2 Follow instructions in paragraphs 1-2 of **Walk 3**

3 Keep ahead along the track then after a few yards follow a path angling RIGHT up through gorse. Soon continue on a green track ahead to where it splits. (For **Walk B** take its right fork to a crossroad of paths/

tracks. Turn right to join the returning route at point **5**.) For **Walk A** take its left fork, then when it bends left keep ahead to cross a green track and follow a clear path ahead up the gorse/heather slopes of Cefn Maen Amor to reach large erratic boulders know as Maen Amor. Continue with the path across the bilberry/heather terrain. Later take its left fork towards the quarry on Tal-y-fan and on towards Maen Penddu standing stone now visible. *This flat-topped stone, almost 2 metres high, and an almost buried stone circle nearby, date from the 2nd millennium BC and were of likely ceremonial importance.* Turn RIGHT up the part stony track, soon levelling out and passing a track leading to the hillside quarry. Soon the green track descends towards an expansive wide valley.

At a tree turn LEFT to cross a footbridge over another stream. Follow it RIGHT to cross a larger footbridge and go across the dam of the second reservoir, then go up a rough green track. Follow it across heather terrain to join the green track left earlier. Follow it towards the Great Orme, shortly crossing higher ground – *with new views east* – then descending to a crossroad of green tracks/ paths. Turn LEFT.

5 Follow the faint green track down to a wall corner. Continue beside it, then turn RIGHT to follow the waymarked North Wales Path across open country and down to join a wall. After the next wall corner the NWP follows a green track down past a side valley, then rises steadily to a ladder-stile/gate. Here follow the stony track up the hillside. At the wall corner turn LEFT.

6 Follow a path alongside the wall, soon descending. It briefly levels out then descends again. Follow a path RIGHT then another on the left up to visit a nearby stone cairn. Return to the first path and follow it down through gorse then bracken to join a green cross-track. Follow it RIGHT then after 30 yards take a path angling back on the left, then another leading RIGHT to the small rocky top of Craigyfedwen. Take a nearby path down to rejoin the track. Follow it down to join your outward route, then follow either the track or lakeside path back to the start.

4 Keep down its right fork, soon bending down the hillside towards reservoirs. After the green track bends right, either keep with the track, or take a path on the left down towards the reservoirs. Cross the stream and go past the first lilly covered reservoir.

5

WALK 5

ST CELYNIN'S CHURCH & TAL Y FAN

DESCRIPTION A choice of routes exploring a fascinating scenic upland landscape, full of antiquity, featuring a remote ancient church, Maen Penddu and other standing stones, an ancient burial chamber, hillfort, a section of Roman road, combined with panoramic views. The main 7 mile walk (**A**) includes an exhilarating climb along the ridge of Taly y Fan, at just under 2000 feet, Snowdonia's most northerly mountain. Although not a difficult ascent, this is for experienced walkers and should be avoided in poor visibility. Allow about 5 hours. Lower level alternative 5½ mile (**B**) and 6½ mile (**C**) walks are included.

START Rowen [SH 761719].

DIRECTIONS Rowen is signposted from the B5106. There is roadside parking near the first house.

Rowen, one of the prettiest villages in the Conwy Valley, stands on an ancient highway, used by Romans then drovers. It once had several mills and inns, but only the Ty Gwyn remains.

I Walk through the village past the Ty Gwyn Hotel, attractive stone houses and a chapel. On the bend turn RIGHT on a signposted path along a lane to a farm. Go through the gate ahead, down the field to the bottom left-hand corner to cross a ladder-stile beyond. Turn RIGHT along a stony track and on the bend cross a ladder-stile ahead. Go along the field edge to another ladder-stile, then follow the raised path up alongside a fence to a narrow road. Follow it RIGHT, then take a signposted path up an access lane on the left past Lwynonn. Later as bends right to a farm cross a ladder-stile ahead. Go along the right-hand bank of the stream, then cross it and follow the wall on your left up to a waymarked gate in it. Turn RIGHT over the stream then head across to Dodre'r coed cottage. At its entrance turn LEFT up a track, soon bearing RIGHT to a

gate above the cottage. The track now rises steadily up the open, then part-wooded hillside. After a small stream, the track bends left then right. About 70 yards further, follow a waymarked path angling RIGHT to cross a nearby ladder-stile/stream and up the tree-covered slope into a field. Continue up to a gate between an outbuilding and a ruined cottage. Pass behind the ruin and go up a path.

2 After about 10 yards, the route turns sharp LEFT past a hawthorn tree. (First follow the wide path ahead to a nearby superb viewpoint.) Follow the improving path up beneath bracken and gorse, then beside a wall up to a ladder-stile. Go along the left-hand side of the small ridge ahead, then across a reedy area, and past another small ridge, with a ruin to your left. Continue along the field, with the church now visible, to a ladder-stile in the top left-hand corner. Go along a green track, then at track junction turn RIGHT to reach the church entrance. *St Celynin's church is a delightfully simple building, whose nave dates from the 14thC. Summer services and harvest thanksgiving are still held here. In the south corner of the churchyard is a rectangular well, renowned for its power to heal sick children. Near the churchyard gate once stood an inn which served travellers crossing the mountains.* Return along the track and past a ladder-stile. When it bends right go through a gate ahead and follow a narrow green track up past a nearby house – *soon with a view of Tal-y-fan ahead* – to a gate into Open Access land by sheepfolds. Go through another gate ahead and follow the green track across open country.

3 After about 150 yards as the track rises half-left you have a choice:
For **Walk B** continue up the green track curving round the western side of Craig Celynin. About midway, the track bears half-RIGHT, rising gently, then after a stream becomes a path, which continues alongside the wall ahead. After passing a small triangular enclosure, bear RIGHT – *the mound on your right is Caer Bach, a 1st millennium BC hillfort* – and follow the old wall on your

Maen Penddu

Maen Penddu

St Celynin's Church

Craig Celynin

burial chamber

N

0   ¼
mile

ROWEN
Inn

P.O.

hostel

burial chamber

standing stones

continue ahead down the slope to join Walk B at the old wall near Cae Bach hillfort.)

left up to a gate. Keep alongside the wall to cross two ladder-stiles, then follow the main path, later rejoining the wall to cross another ladder-stile. Follow the green track down to go through two gates below Cae Coch, then cross a ladder-stile onto a track. Turn LEFT and resume instructions at paragraph **5**.

For **Walk A** take a path angling away on the right through heather and gorse to cross a stream between two wall corners. Take the path close by the wall on your right -(the other is an alternative route to Maen Penddu as shown.) Follow it across open upland pasture, later turning sharp LEFT up a green track across the gorse-covered pasture towards Tal y Fan, to reach Maen Penddu. *This large flat-topped stone, almost 2 metres high, and an almost buried stone circle nearby, date from the 2nd millennium BC and were likely of ceremonial importance.* Here, turn LEFT and follow a path to cross a stream by the second of two ruins. The path now rises and continues alongside a wall. As the wall begins to gently curve follow a path straight ahead. After about 100 yards the ground begins to descend. (For **Walk C**

4 For **Walk A**, angle RIGHT across the boulder-covered slope to join a well-used path heading directly up the mountain, about 100 yards from a ruin to your left. At the top of the slope, the path briefly bears right, then continues across a depression on the NE side of the mountain before rising to the wall on the Tal y Fan ridge. A good path follows the wall west along the undulating rocky ridge, past a ladder-stile accessing the summit trig point, then shortly begins a long initially steep descent to cross a ladder-stile at the bwlch. Now follow the occasionally waymarked, stiled path down the southern slopes of Tal y Fan to a road. Turn LEFT and on the bend continue ahead along a track to the entrance to Cae Coch.

5 Now follow the old enclosed green lane, soon on a steady descent, to reach the Youth Hostel, then continue down the steep road into Rowen. *The lane is an ancient route, which later became part of the Roman road from Canovium fort in the Conwy valley to Segontium fort at Caernarfon. On the adjoining slopes are 2nd millennium BC standing stones and Maen y Bard Neolithic burial chamber.*

WALK 6
LLYN CRAFNANT & LLYN GEIRIONYDD

DESCRIPTION A 5¼ mile walk (**A**) visiting two popular beautiful scenic upland lakes, enclosed by hills and mountains, or an easy 3 mile circuit of Llyn Crafnant (**B**), featuring a seasonal lakeside café. The route follows a waymarked forestry trail along the northern side of Llyn Crafnant and beyond, then joins the valley road. **Walk A** takes a waymarked forestry trail up across a forested ridge and down into the adjoining valley. It then follows a path, uneven in part due to exposed tree roots, along the western side of Llyn Geirionydd, or an equally enjoyable lakeside road alternative, Afterwards it follows a waymarked undulating trail across part-wooded slopes past an old slate mine and down to the start. Allow about 3½ hours. An alternative 2 mile circuit of Llyn Geirionydd can be enjoyed starting from the lakeside car park.
START Crafnant Forestry car park [SH 756618].
DIRECTIONS From the centre of Trefriw, take the road signposted to Llyn Crafnant opposite Gwesty Fairy Falls Hotel. Follow the narrow road up past junctions for nearly 2 miles to reach the car park/toilets.

1 From the Gwydyr Forest information board near toilets follow the nearby waymarked yellow trail along the track, then up through trees to the road. Continue up the road above the Afon Crafnant to reach the end of the lake. *Just ahead is a monument erected in 1896 by inhabitants of Llanrwst to commemorate the gift by Richard James of the lake, created into a reservoir for the town.* Turn RIGHT on the waymarked yellow trail across the lake's outlet then follow the stony forestry track along the northern side of the lake. *Llyn Crafnant, ¾ mile long, means 'lake in the valley of garlic'. It contains rainbow and wild brown trout, making*

it popular with fishermen. Later keep to the lower waymarked left fork to pass the end of the lake. Shortly, the track becomes a stony path which rises steadily to a waymarked path junction.

2 Here, take the yellow trail left fork down through trees to a ladder-stile. Just below, the path angles LEFT and descends through conifers to cross a footbridge over the stream by Hendre Bach. Turn LEFT, go through a gate and across a stream, then follow the track down beneath a house and on past Tan-y-Manod to join the gated end of the valley road. Follow the narrow road past a house, soon with good views along the lake, then Pen-y-Llyn and Cornel. (For **Walk B** continue along the road past Cynllwyd Mawr, with its lakeside cafe.)

3 At a derelict stone building just before a telephone box, take the waymarked blue trail angling up on the right to a kissing gate and on up the edge of woodland. Just beyond a stream, at a ladder-stile, the blue trail bends sharp RIGHT and rises in stages through conifers. The path eventually levels out and passes through a wall gap, then descends to the bend of a stony forestry track. Keep ahead down the track and at the track junction bend RIGHT. After a few yards, at a blue trail waymark post, take a path on the left down through trees to rejoin the forestry track. The path continues opposite (if muddy use the track), crosses the track again, and descends to rejoin the forestry track. Follow it down towards Llyn Geirionydd.

4 On the bend cross a stile by a gate ahead. (Alternatively, keep with the track, follow the road alongside the lake, then take a track across its outlet to the monument at point **5**.) Follow the path beneath the cottage then on to the edge of Llyn Geirionydd and a stile at the wood corner. The path keeps close to the wooded edge of the lake, later climbing a small rocky spur above a corner of the lake, before descending near a fence enclosing an old mine to continue along the lakeside. After a stile, keep ahead, then follow a waymarked path alongside a low wall

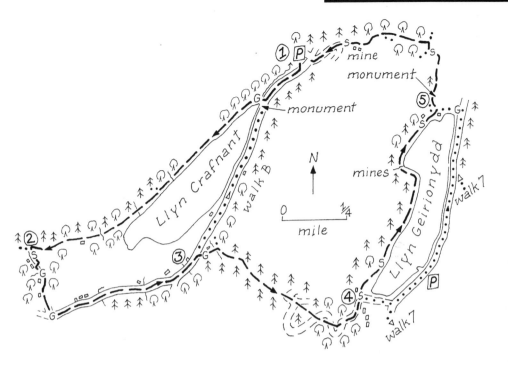

to to reach a track beyond a stone building. Go up to the nearby monument – *erected in 1850 to commemorate the reputed birthplace of Talisien, a 6thC Chief Bard. It was toppled in a 1976 storm, then re-erected in 1994. In summer, parties of Victorian visitors came here, often entertained by music and sports. Between 1863-1922, an annual poetry/musical event, first established by local poet Gwilym Cowyld, was held at the monument.*

5 Descend its far side to join a wide green path by a Trefriw Trails 5 waymark post. Follow it past conifers, then angle down through a gap in an old wall. Descend the stony path to a ladder-stile and at a path junction beyond turn RIGHT on the way-marked trail. Soon take the waymarked left fork across the part-wooded slope to a wall-gap. The trail path now rises to a waymark post at a path junction, where it bears RIGHT and briefly rises before continuing across the part tree and bracken covered hillside to

Llyn Crafnant monument

reach an old slate mine site – *which operated from the 18thC until the early 20thC. Continue down the path to the bend of a forestry track and follow it down to the road by the car park.*

WALK 7

GWYDYR LAKES

DESCRIPTION A 5½ mile walk (**A**), with extensive views, exploring an area of Gwydyr Forest Park featuring numerous scenic upland lakes that once provided water for the lead-mines. The route first follows a waymarked yellow forest trail in reverse to near Llyn Glangors, then continues down across upland pasture and along the eastern shore of Llyn Geirionydd. After diverting to Llyn Bodgynydd, it then rejoins the forest trail. Allow about 3½ hours. Also included is the full 2½ mile waymarked yellow forest trail in reverse (**B**), and an optional additional ¾ mile walk (**C**) to the 19thC Llanrwst mine engine house and Llyn Sarnau.
START Llyn Sarnau car park [SH 778592].
DIRECTIONS Follow directions in Walk 12 to Hafna mine car park, then continue up the road past Nant-B.H. Outdoor Education Centre to reach a car park on the left by Llyn Sarnau.

I From the information board at the far end of the car park cross the road to the start of the Forest Lakes Walk opposite and follow the yellow trail up into the trees. Soon, when the waymarked trail turns left keep ahead. The path rises steadily, then descends to a stream, and rises again. When it levels out at a path junction bend RIGHT with the way-marked path, briefly descending then continuing through mature woodland. At a waymarked path junction just before a signposted viewpoint, the trail bends LEFT to a nearby forestry track. Follow it RIGHT.

2 After several bends, turn LEFT off the track past a waymark post and follow the yellow trail up through a clearing scarred by mining and on to reach another stony forestry track. Follow it LEFT past a small lake, then turn RIGHT down the trail path and on between the first lake and a larger one. *These attractive lily-covered lakes, a habitat for dragonflies, are known as the Three Dams Reservoir.* The path continues along the larger lake's northern side and on through trees to reach a forestry track. Follow it RIGHT – *soon enjoying a view of Llyn Glangors* – to reach a

waymark post. (For **Walk B** turn LEFT down the yellow trail towards Llyn Glangors. The path then bends – *now with a view of another lake ahead* – and continues through trees, soon bending down to the end of a forestry track. Follow it past the tree-lined lake and on to seats at point **5**.)

3 About 75 yards further along the track, turn sharp LEFT down a signed path to a ladder-stile near Llyn Glangors. Go across the end of the lake to a stile and up to a telegraph pole. Go down the slope, past another tele-graph pole, to a ladder-stile. Continue ahead, soon passing a further telegraph pole, then descending to a ladder-stile. Continue to a track by the lower of two concrete buildings on the site of the former New Pandora lead mine. Turn RIGHT up the track, then at the second building, turn LEFT to go through a gate in the fence on your right. Continue to a nearby ladder-stile, then follow the path across the part heather covered terrain – *soon with the sight of Llyn Geirionydd below.* The path makes a long steady descent to the lake-side road.

4 Turn LEFT and follow the road along the eastern side of the lake, past a slip-way and car park/toilets. *Llyn Geirionydd is said to be the home of the 6thC poet Talisien. Trees were planted here in 1929 to soften the landscape scarred by intensive mining in the 1870s. The car park stands on the waste tip and the adjacent mine level were part of the New Pandora mine complex. Lead was taken by tramway along the eastern shore of the lake then by aerial ropeway to Klondike lead mill mine 250 feet below.* After passing the end of the lake the road turns up a side valley. Later it passes spoil heaps and a track leading to Ty'n-y-Groes, then a signposted path into a forest. About 40 yards further go across a small parking area on your right to a waymarked Open Access gateway into Cors Bodgynyd Nature Reserve. Follow the stony path past a delightful small lake and an old mine to reach Llyn Bodgynyd – *a reservoir for the Pandora lead-mine.* The path continues along its southern edge. Opposite a tiny island on the wooded shoreline is a seat. Return to the road and take an unsigned path opposite up through mixed woodland to a forestry track where you rejoin the yellow trail. Turn RIGHT past seats at a good viewpoint.

5 Continue along the stony track. Later on a bend at a fenced-off mine and a green forestry post, turn LEFT up an old green track and on to reach another stony forestry track. Follow it RIGHT past a house and at a track junction keep ahead. At another track junction turn LEFT up the track. Just beyond the next bend turn RIGHT on the yellow trail past a waymark post then take the left fork past another post down to join your outward route.

Walk **C** From the car park entrance go along the nearby stony forestry track to a ladder-stile on the left. Go up the path, then turn RIGHT to reach a waymarked path junction. Take the left fork to the Llanrwst mine engine house and on to a ladder-stile. Turn RIGHT down the forestry track, then LEFT down an old narrow track opposite a gate/ladder-stile. Shortly, turn RIGHT down a narrow path to join a stony track. Follow it RIGHT past Llyn Sarnau back to the start.

Llyn Bodgynydd

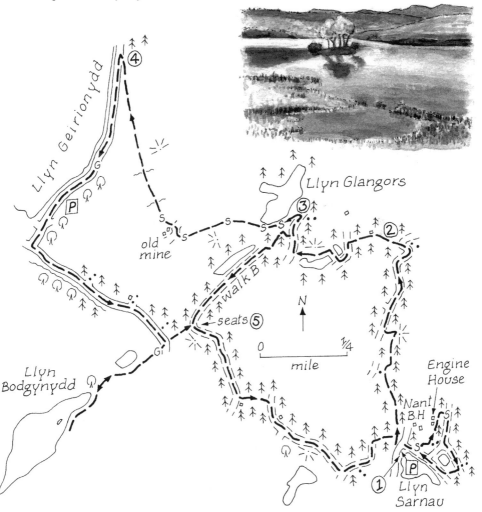

WALK 8

LLYN ELSI

DESCRIPTION A 6 mile walk (**A**) exploring the attractive part-wooded upland area above Betws-y-Coed containing the beautiful hidden lake of Llyn Elsi. The route follows a waymarked white forestry trail up to Llyn Elsi, then follows the trail in reverse around the lake. After enjoying extensive views from the commemorative monument, the route meanders down through old quarry workings and woodland to cross the Miners Bridge for a delightful riverside return. Allow about 3½ hours. The route can be shortened to a 4¾ mile walk (**B**) by going direct to the monument.

START Car park by toilets, near the railway station, Betws-y-Coed [SH 795565] – both signposted from the main A5 road.

From the southern end of the car park follow a pathway past the toilets to cross the main road. Turn RIGHT past the PO/stores, then LEFT up a road, soon bearing RIGHT beneath Church Hill House and above St Mary's church. At a Gwydr Forest Park information board, marking the start of two forestry trails, head up to a barrier gate into the wood. Now follow the waymarked white/blue trails up a stony forestry track. Later when the track splits, continue up the RIGHT fork on the waymarked white trail. Follow the trail through several track junctions up to a bend overlooking Llyn Elsi, with a good view of Moel Siabod. (For **Walk B** turn right and follow the waymarked stony trail path up to the monument above the lake.)

2 The main walk now follows the track LEFT along the eastern side of the lake. Just beyond the end of the lake the track descends. When it bends left, go past a waymark post on the right up a stony path. Follow the undulating trail path, soon heading north through an area of birch. After crossing a turning area continue along a forestry track – *with a brief view of Llyn Elsi.* Shortly the track bends west towards Moel Siabod, where it overlooks a narrow arm of the lake. Here, at a waymark post on the right go down the stony trail path to cross a foot-

bridge and continue near the water's edge to reach a prominent viewpoint across the lake – *a good place to stop to watch the wildfowl and dragonflies.* The path now meanders round the western side of the lake to the dam. Here go up steps and descend to a footbridge over the lake's outlet to reach a path junction below the dam. Keep ahead and follow the stony path up to a monument and seats. *It was erected to commemorate the opening of the Betws-y-Coed waterworks in 1914, when the lake became a reservoir providing water for the town. There are good views from Moel Siabod to the Carneddau mountains.* Return down the path.

3 At the bottom of the slope, turn RIGHT along a waymarked path through an area of small trees to a forestry track. Go down a path opposite through another area of small trees, then alongside a wall, to a ladder-stile. Follow the signed path to an old track with a stone barn visible ahead. Here turn sharp RIGHT and follow another signed path down the track to cross a stile by a barn. Turn LEFT down the path, through an old gateway and down through trees to a ladder-stile. Continue down the path past the former 19thC Hafod-las slate quarry, soon bending right. After 50 yards, at a gate at the end of the wall on the right turn LEFT along a former tramway.

4 At a facing gate, descend a path to cross a stream leading from a mine adit, and continue between spoil heaps and past two small quarry buildings. Just beyond the second building, descend the path to cross a stile on the left. Go up the field edge by nearby spoil heaps to a stile into a wood. Follow the path through the trees to reach a track. Follow it LEFT. At a track junction below a house keep ahead on the track to cross a stream. About 100 yards further, at a large rock slab turn RIGHT down a path towards the nearby small waterfall, then continue down through the wood, initially near the stream to a small parking area. Turn RIGHT down the minor road past houses to the A5. Follow the signposted path opposite, soon descending steps to cross the Miners Bridge – *just as miners would have done on their way to work in the lead-mines during the 19thC.*

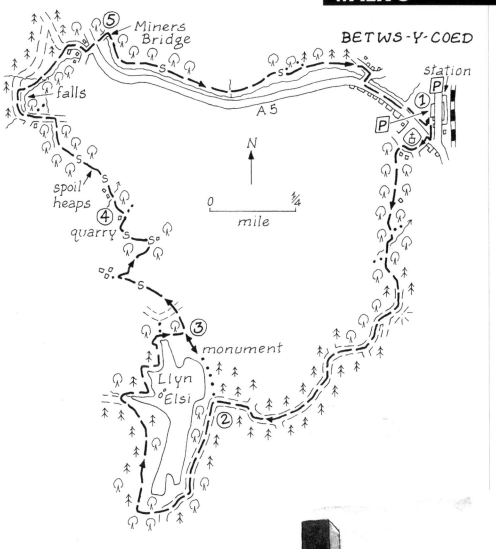

BETWS-Y-COED

station

falls

Miners Bridge

A5

N

0 ——————— ¼

mile

spoil heaps

④ quarry

③ monument

Llyn Elsi

②

①

5 Turn RIGHT alongside the fence and follow the riverside path along the edge of a wood then a long field. After a ladder-stile into another wood you reach a picnic area. Either continue close by the river or follow the wide path, soon boardwalked and raised, to join the road by toilets and a car park. Follow the road across the bridge (Pont-y-Pair), then turn LEFT along the main road. Just past the Royal Oak Hotel, take a path through the park back to the start.

Llyn Elsi monument

WALK 9

UPPER MACHNO VALLEY

DESCRIPTION A 5½ mile (**A**) or 5 mile (**B**) walk around the upper Machno valley. The route first follows a forestry track around the lower slopes of Moel Pen-y-bryn past several good viewpoints, then descends a path through the forest. Walk A continues on paths down to Cwm Penmachno village, then follows the valley road east to pass through Carrog. Walk B heads east then descends to the valley road. Both walks then follow the river along the attractive valley. Allow about 3½ hours.

START Car park, Coed Pen-y-bryn [SH 786497].

DIRECTIONS From Penmachno follow the road south towards Cwm Penmachno. After ½ mile you reach the wide entrance to Coed Pen-y-bryn. The car park lies a little way up the stony forestry track.

1 Follow the stony forestry track up to a junction at a good viewpoint, then continue ahead up the track. Follow it for 1¼ miles past viewpoints and a track on the left to reach a crossroad of tracks. Turn LEFT on the signposted red bike trail, shortly descending, then take a waymarked path on the left down through conifers to another stony track. The path continues opposite through the forest gradually descending to another stony track. (For **Walk B** turn left and follow instructions in paragraph **2** of Walk 5 to the road. After crossing the bridge over the river go through an iron gate on the left then follow instructions in paragraph **3**.)

2 For **Walk A** take the waymarked path ahead through mature trees, past an old ruin and down the forest edge to a stile. Follow the path down the middle of the field to a ladder-stile and footbridge over the stream. Go up the slope ahead and bear LEFT down the field edge to a gate at the back of houses to reach the nearby road in Cwm Penmachno. Follow the road LEFT out of the village to the junction at Carrog.

Continue east along the valley road. Just before it bends across a bridge over the river, go through an iron gate on the right.

3 Go along the field's right hand edge to a gate by a stream. Keep ahead across the next large field to another gate, then follow a farm track to Pen-y-bedw. Go past outbuildings and the house then down its access track. Just before it crosses a bridge over the river, turn RIGHT on a signposted path. Go along a wide initially reedy old green lane to a gate above the river. Go along the walled track, through another gate at sheep pens, then an adjoining small gate on the left. Turn RIGHT across a small fenced area to a nearby gate and continue across the slope to pass a wall corner with a bridge over the river nearby. Go along the raised edge of the next field, soon joining a nearby farm track to go through a gate ahead. Follow the green track to another gate, then continue along the edge of a reedy stream to cross a large footbridge over the river – *a great place to stop* – and a nearby ladder-stile onto the road. Continue along the road to the entrance to Coed-Pen-y-bryn.

Footbridge over Afon Machno

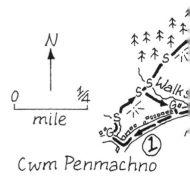

Cwm Penmachno

WALK 10

CWM PENMACHNO

DESCRIPTION A 3 mile walk around the upper Machno valley near the former quarrying village of Cwm Penmachno. The route rises on field paths to the forest edge then continues east before descending to the valley road, which it follows back through Carrog to the village.
START Cwm Penmachno [SH 757476].
DIRECTIONS Follow the valley road to Cwm Penmachno to find roadside parking adjoining a gap in houses.

Cwm Penmachno was once a bustling Welsh-speaking slate quarry community, with many shops, chapels, a church, pub and a school. Quarrying began at Rhiw bach in the early 19th C and continued at other upland quarries until the last closed in 1962. In the 1880s 130 men worked at Rhiw bach, so remote that it built houses for families, barracks for men, a shop and schoolroom/chapel.

edge to a ladder-stile then up the next field edge to a waymarked fence corner. Continue down the field edge to cross a ladder-stile. Turn LEFT down to cross a nearby footbridge and ladder-stile. Follow the path up the middle of the field to a stile in the top corner, then up the edge of the forest, past a stone ruin and on up to a forestry track. Turn RIGHT.

2 Follow the track to a turning area. Here do a sharp U-turn RIGHT down a waymarked path, soon bending LEFT and continuing along an old rough track through a clearing. At the end of the track turn LEFT up a wide path into the forest. After a few yards it bears RIGHT across two streams, then another (large pipe) at the forest edge. Go up the slope to a hidden stile then across the mid-slopes of the reedy field to a gate in the fence ahead.

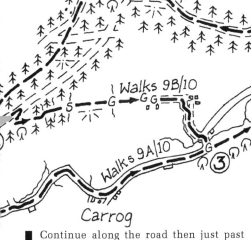

Cross the stream beyond and follow a faint green track along the edge of two fields, through a gate then past a nearby barn to a gate ahead. Pass to the left of the house and go along its access track to a cattle grid. Continue down the track, soon bending RIGHT over another cattle grid past nearby Llechwedd Hafod farm. Follow the stony access track down to the road. Turn RIGHT across the bridge over the river and continue along the road to Carrog. Take the road towards Cwm Penmachno, later passing an impressive chapel and crossing over the river to return to the start

Continue along the road then just past single story terraced cottages turn RIGHT up a side road. On the bend by buildings go through a gate on the right. Go up the field

WALK II
CWM EIDDA

DESCRIPTION A 7½ mile walk from Penmachno to Cwm Eidda for experienced hill walkers, offering extensive views. The route climbs in stages into open rough upland pasture, crosses a broad ridge (1148 feet/350 metres), then descends to a minor road in Cwm Eidda. From Eidda Fawr farm you have a choice of routes up to the bwlch, before a splendid descent on an old drovers' road to Penmachno. **Route a** follows a waymarked path across rough upland pasture. **Route b** continues along the road to join the old drovers' road earlier. Allow about 5 hours.

START War memorial/Churchyard, Penmachno [SH 790505].

I Follow the road over the river and past the former Machno Inn. Bend left with the main road, then take a signposted path on the right between terraced houses to a kissing gate. Follow the enclosed stony path up to a minor road. Go to the track opposite, then cross a stile up on the right. Go up the field edge to a ladder-stile. At a waymarked telegraph pole ahead angle LEFT up the field to a ladder-stile and continue up to a stile/gate by a cottage. Go past the end of the cottage to a ladder-stile. Go up the slope ahead and on to a small waymarked gate in the corner. Go up the field edge to a stile and through a gap in the boundary beyond. Turn RIGHT and follow the fenced topped embanked boundary across the tussocky upland pasture of Y Foel – *enjoying extensive views* – and down to a gate onto an access track. Go along a green track opposite to a stile.

2 Follow the fence on your left to join an access lane. After crossing the stream turn RIGHT to a nearby small wooden gate. Head up the field to a ladder-stile in its right hand corner. Angle LEFT up the slope, then go up a short farm track. Continue up the reedy/tussocky terrain, soon passing about 40 yards below the forest perimeter fence corner, then go across the right hand edge of a flattish area beneath high ground. At the

remains of a stone structure turn RIGHT past the short embanked boundary up to a stile into the forest. Turn LEFT, soon bending RIGHT and rising through trees to reach a waymark post at the bend of a forestry track, with a bench seat nearby. Keep ahead along the narrowing green track to a small gate into open country. Angle LEFT across the part reedy covered terrain, soon rising across the gorse covered slope to a stone stile in the wall ahead.

3 Cross the stile and keep ahead to pass along the base of the small gorse-covered slope, then follow the path across the tussocky terrain towards a rocky hillock. When it fades angle RIGHT up and across the tussocky ground, then along the right hand edge of flattish ground, passing beneath rocky crags and high ground. Continue across a tussocky/reedy area to a stile in a fence. Keep ahead along the edge of reedy terrain, gradually descending on an intermittent path across a wettish reedy area, then go up green pasture ahead. Now, with a gate ahead, angle RIGHT to a stile in the fence visible on the skyline. Continue down the next field to a stile between strips of woodland. Cross the small ridge ahead, descend to another stile and cross the stream. Angle RIGHT across the field to a stile and descend the next field – *enjoying good views into Cwm Eidda* – to a stile/gate in the bottom left-hand corner. Turn LEFT down the field edge to a waymarked gate. Go down the field to a stile/gate by a stream. Continue down the edge of the next two fields onto a minor road. Follow it RIGHT along Cwm Eidda past Ty Uchaf to reach Eidda Fawr farm. (For **Route b** continue along the road, then when it bends left to Pont Blaen-Eidda turn right up a rough track. Follow it to cross Pont Rhyd-yr-halen, then up across rough pasture to point **5**.)

16

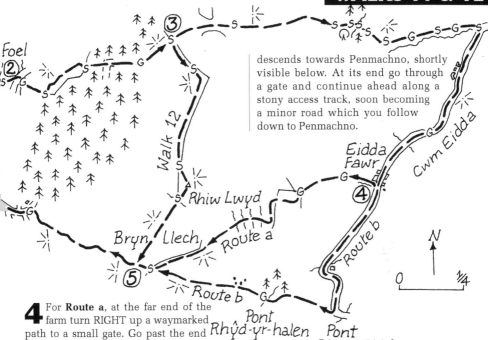

descends towards Penmachno, shortly visible below. At its end go through a gate and continue ahead along a stony access track, soon becoming a minor road which you follow down to Penmachno.

4 For **Route a**, at the far end of the farm turn RIGHT up a waymarked path to a small gate. Go past the end of the large barn and up the reedy right bank of the stream through trees into open country. Continue along the left hand embanked edge of a sunken reedy track to a facing gate by a ruin. Continue beside the fence above the old track up into rough upland pasture. After a gate keep ahead beside the wall to a gate in it, then turn RIGHT across the tussocky ground to a waymark post on an old embanked boundary. Walk LEFT along the old boundary, then after about 200 yards, as it begins a gentle descent, follow a clear path leading RIGHT towards the distant trig point on Rhiw Lwyd. It then heads to a visible waymark post and continues across the tussocky terrain up to another post on the skyline at a good viewpoint. Keep ahead past a waymark post at the fence corner, then follow the fence across tussocky ground to a ladder-stile/gate to join a green track at the bwlch. Go up the track, soon levelling out – *enjoying extensive views of Snowdon and other mountains, and along Cwm Penmachno.*

5 The track – *part of an old drovers' route from Anglesey via Penmachno and Ysbyty Ifan to Mid-Wales* – now steadily

WALK 12
RHIW LWYD

DESCRIPTION A 4¼ mile walk (**B**) for experienced hill walkers, rising in stages to a broad ridge of Open Access land featuring Rhiw Lwyd (1305 feet/398 metres), offering panoramic views and returning down an old drovers' route. Allow about 3 hours.
START As Walk 11.

1-2 Follow instructions in paragraphs **1 & 2** of Walk 11.

3 Follow the wall up past a higher stone stile onto a small rocky top offering all-round views. Descend to follow the nearby fence south across the rough upland pasture to cross a stile in it, then angle RIGHT to the trig point on Rhiw Lwyd. Descend south to a stile then continue across the broad tussocky ridge, then the flattish top of Bryn Llech to join a track at the bwlch. Follow instructions in paragraph **5** of Walk 11.

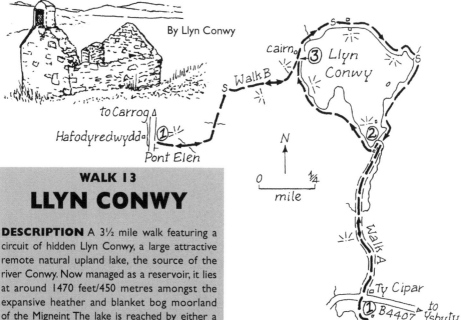

By Llyn Conwy

WALK 13
LLYN CONWY

DESCRIPTION A 3½ mile walk featuring a circuit of hidden Llyn Conwy, a large attractive remote natural upland lake, the source of the river Conwy. Now managed as a reservoir, it lies at around 1470 feet/450 metres amongst the expansive heather and blanket bog moorland of the Migneint The lake is reached by either a stony access track (**Walk A**) or by a footpath (**Walk B**). The clockwise lake circuit, which follows intermittent paths through predominantly rough heather terrain, is for experienced hill walkers and should be avoided in poor visibility. Walk A includes a visit to nearby delightful waterfalls. Allow about 2½ hours.
START Ty Cipar [SH 781446] or Pont Elen [SH 765457].
DIRECTIONS Ty Cipar lies on the B4407, 5 miles from Ysbyty Ifan. Pont Ellen lies on a minor road accessible from both the B4407 and Carrog in the Penmachno valley.

1 For **Walk A** first head south across open ground down to visit the waterfalls on the Afon Conwy, then return. From Ty Cipar follow the stony track north across the vast heather moorland to eventually reach Llyn Conwy near a boathouse.

2 Head south to the nearby small ruined dwelling – *once used overnight by fishermen* – then follow a faint path along the western edge of the lake. After about 250 yards the path angles away from the lake and crosses high ground ahead, passing a small stone structure to your left. The faint path continues down to the lake then close along

its edge. Shortly head up to a nearby old waymark post below a stone cairn to join a better path.

3 Follow the path around the lake's north western corner to a ladder-stile, then to an old boathouse. Continue near the rocky shore and on to a stile at its north eastern corner. Go along the lake's eastern side past a nearby small island, after which a path continues a little way from the lake, then bends to a handrailed footbridge. Continue to the stony access track.

Walk B

1 Follow the signposted path up the rough open pasture near the boundary. Just before a fence corner the path bears LEFT, crosses a stream/ reedy area, then continues up near the fence to a ladder-stile. Angle RIGHT then follow a gently rising path, vague in places, eastwards. Shortly the path bends north-eastwards and descends towards Llyn Conwy to an old waymark post below a stone cairn. Now follow instructions in paragraphs **3** and **2** of Walk A to complete a circuit of the lake.

WALK 14
BRYN DDU & ABERGLASLYN PASS

DESCRIPTION A 3¼ mile walk exploring the beautiful varied scenery near the picturesque village of Beddgelert. The route first visits famous Gelert's Grave, then follows a way-marked National Trust path up to a tower on the small hill of Bryn Ddu (603 ft/184 metres) offering panoramic views, and down through Coed Aberglaslyn to the A498. It returns alongside the river Glaslyn passing through the stunning wooded Aberglaslyn Pass, for part of the way near the narrow gauge Welsh Highland Railway. Allow about 2 hours.
START Beddgelert SH 590481.

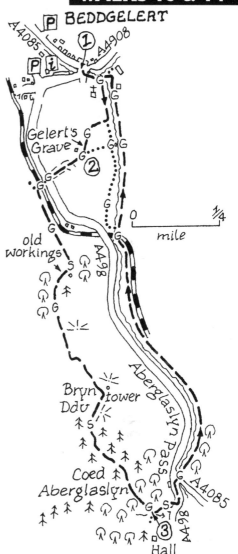

1 From the village bridge, take the riverside lane signposted to Gelert's grave/toilets. Just before the footbridge, go through a gate and follow the wide riverside path south. Shortly, turn RIGHT to follow another path to Gelert's grave and on to a ruin containing a bronze sculpture of the dog. *The 'legend' is said to have been created in the late 18thC by a local hotel landlord to attract tourists – and it seems to have worked!*

2 Go through a small gate ahead and follow the National Trust path, then track, to the A498. Take the National Trust path opposite up to cross the railway line. Follow the path to a gate, then along the next field edge to a ladder-stile. The waymarked path passes old workings, rises to a small gate, then climbs to Bryn Ddu tower and a ladder-stile, before descending through Coed Aberglaslyn to a small gate onto a path junction.

3 Turn LEFT and follow the path down to the A498. Follow it LEFT to the junction and cross over the bridge. *Until the early 19thC Aberglaslyn was a small tidal port boasting copper exporting and boat building.* From a kissing gate on the left follow a path above the river, later near the Welsh Highland Railway. After crossing it, continue along the river's right bank to Beddgelert.

The original Welsh Highland railway opened in 1923 connecting Caernarfon with Porthmadog via a standard gauge transfer at Dinas. The goods and passenger railway was abandoned in 1937. After a long and controversial campaign from the 1960s, followed by much voluntary effort and grant funding, the railway was fully restored in 2011. It now offers a spectacular 25 mile steam locomotive hauled journey through the heart of Snowdonia.

CWM BYCHAN & CWM NANMOR

DESCRIPTION An 8 mile walk of great variety, featuring contrasting upland valleys, a beautiful lake, woodland, mining relics and extensive views. The route climbs steadily up Cwm Bychan which was mined for copper from the late 18thC until 1930, and contained an ore-processing plant. It passes the remains of an aerial ropeway, reaching a height of 951 ft/290 metres, before descending to continue alongside Llyn Dinas. After rising across open country, it follows a quiet upland road, then paths through the attractive wooded Nanmor valley, before returning to Nantmor. Allow about 5 hours.

START National Trust Aberglaslyn car park, Nantmor SH 597462 or roadside car park near Llyn Dinas SH 612494.

DIRECTIONS The pay & display car park lies off the A4085, near Nantmor. The alternative A488 roadside car park is just before Llyn Dinas, 1½ miles from Beddgelert.

I Go through a small gate by the ticket machine and toilets. Turn RIGHT signposted Cwm Bychan to pass under the railway bridge. Go past picnic tables and up to a cross path. Follow it RIGHT up through woodland and on to a small gate. The path briefly accompanies the stream, then rises steadily up Cwm Bychan, later passing aerial ropeway pylons and a former copper mine. Keep ahead, rising steadily past a ruin and waste tip on your right, later becoming more enclosed by heather/boulder covered ridges. Cross a ladder-stile at the highest point – *with views of Snowdon, Moel Siabod, and Cnicht.* Follow the path LEFT to a finger post at the top of Grib Ddu. Turn RIGHT down the stony path signposted to Llyn Dinas. The path begins a long steady descent, later levelling out, before a final steeper descent to Llyn Dinas.

2 Turn RIGHT along the lakeside path, over a stream and on to a ladder-stile. Take the waymarked path up through heather,

bracken then trees, and down to a ladder-stile just beyond a ruin. Continue down the path, over a stream and on by the fence to cross a ladder-stile over it. Follow the path up across the wooded slope, soon taking its right fork to pass above a ruin. After a ladder-stile the path rises to a viewpoint, then descends briefly before rising steadily through bracken. After briefly levelling out – *with a view across to Snowdon and Y Lliwedd* – the path continues up to a ladder-stile then up to another.

3 The path rises through rhododendrons and passes a cottage to a ladder-stile. Turn RIGHT through a wall gap, then follow the path LEFT beside the wall and on across open ground to a ladder-stile/gate at the corner of a small wood. The path now crosses a small rise ahead, then descends to follow a wall over a track and up across higher ground ahead and down to cross a ladder-stile over it. Turn LEFT and follow the path near the wall down and up onto the small ridge ahead. Turn LEFT along its top, then angle RIGHT down past a telegraph pole. At a ladder-stile continue beside the

wall to a gate by Blaen Nant onto a minor road. Follow it RIGHT along the attractive upland valley, past a cottage, then old spoil heaps, now accompanied by the infant Nanmor river. The valley gradually becomes more enclosed.

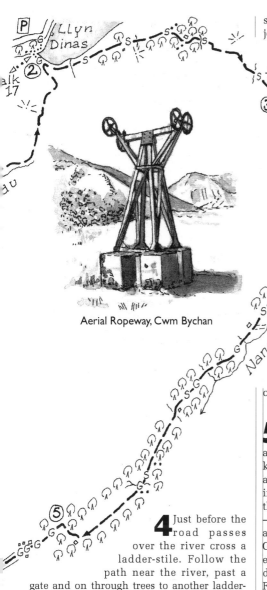

Aerial Ropeway, Cwm Bychan

soon descending to a wall gap and being joined by a path from the left. After a small

tips

gate go ahead through bracken up to join a faint narrow green track. Keep ahead. It soon becomes a wide path, passes through a wall gap and continues along the edge of a large reedy area. It then bends RIGHT across it, meanders up through trees, and continues beside a wall into a field.

5 Just beyond turn LEFT past a telegraph pole to go through a waymarked gate ahead. Go through the narrow field up to a kissing gate and up the next field edge below a house to a waymarked gate by outbuildings. Go through a gate opposite and down the road – *with views of Hebog and the coast* – shortly passing through a gate. Just before a cottage turn RIGHT down to a wall gap. Go down the field, passing close to an old embanked boundary with large tree and ladder, to go through a signed wall gap below. Follow a path near the stream to a kissing gate. Turn RIGHT near the wall, then LEFT along the reedy field edge near a fence to cross streams. Keep ahead past the smaller telegraph pole, then a small rock outcrop to a gate on a lane by stables and Cilfynydd. Go down the lane to a road by a chapel. Follow it RIGHT down through Nantmor, over the railway line, to the A4085. Turn RIGHT back to the car park.

4 Just before the road passes over the river cross a ladder-stile. Follow the path near the river, past a gate and on through trees to another ladder-stile. Continue along the path then go past Buarthau cottage. Follow a path to an old gateway and on to a gate. The path continues along Cwm Nanmor, soon passing through woodland to a gate, then to a ladder-stile/gate. The path now rises through the trees, levels out then passes behind a cottage and crosses a stream. After passing through two wall-gaps, the path rises through woodland,

21

WALK 16
CRAFLWYN

DESCRIPTION A 1½ mile walk, linking sections of National Trust waymarked trails, rising through the attractive woodland of Coed Craflwyn and across upland pasture grazed by wild goats, with panoramic views. About 600 feet of climbing , steep in places, but well worth the effort. Allow about 1¾ hours.
START Craflwyn National Trust car park SH 600490.
DIRECTIONS Craflwyn lies just off the A498 about 1 mile from Beddgelert.

From the information board at the rear of the Warden's office go through a small gateway into Coed Craflwyn, then follow the meandering green trail up past a ruin. At a waymarked path junction just beyond a stream, turn LEFT to continue with the green trail up through the wood, past your yellow return path and through a wall gap. It then rises more steeply to another wall gap, recrosses the stream and continues up to a waymarked green/red trail junction at the wood edge. Follow the green trail LEFT through a nearby wall gap and across the open hillside, soon rising near a wall. Beyond its corner, the path does a sharp U-turn back up to a small gateway in the wall and continues up beside it. When the path levels out divert RIGHT to a great viewpoint. Continue with the green trail to a wall gap and on across the hillside to cross a wall. Just beyond turn LEFT, now on the red trail, to a nearby small gate by a ruin, and on across the hillside to a ladder-stile. The path now rises gently then descends to a wall gap.

2 At the next red/black trail waymark post take the red trail down to a stile. It continues down to pass a large wooden seat at a prominent viewpoint. Later, after a wall gap, the path descends more steeply through trees and another wall gap, then continues down past a side path. At another waymarked path junction, keep ahead to follow the yellow woodland trail through two wall gaps and a stone sheepfold to a small gate, then down to join your outward route.

WALK 17
NANT GWYNANT

DESCRIPTION A varied 7 mile upland and valley walk, with a cafe mid-way. The route follows waymarked National Trust paths up through Coed Craflwyn and across the lower southern slopes of Yr Aran, up through old mine workings to a height of 1115 ft/340 metres, then through a hidden upland valley and down to join the Watkin Path. After descending to Pont Bethania and Gwynant cafe the route returns past Llyn Dinas, then follows the river past Sygun Copper Mine. Allow about 4½ hours.
START Craflwyn National Trust car park. SH 600490 or Pont Bethania SH 628507.

Follow instructions in paragraph 1 of Walk 16.

2 At the next waymark post continue ahead on the black waymarked path. After a ladder-stile, continue with the path, soon parallel with a fence. It then bends left through an old wall, and briefly continues beside it, before moving away and gradually descending to pass to the left of a fence corner. The waymarked path continues to a ladder-stile/gate in the fence by a ruin. Cross a stream ahead and a ladder-stile by a gate on the green track above. Follow the former mine track towards Yr Aran. After a gate it rises steadily, initially near the stream, then becomes a green path.

3 After passing a ruined mine building on the left, the path bends RIGHT up to a stream and continues up a narrow rocky valley, past a waste tip and over a steam. The path briefly levels out then rises onto a narrow ridge ahead – *the highest point of the walk, offering new views of Cwm Gorsen below, Cnicht and Moel Siabod*. Descend to a ladder-stile below. The waymarked path continues down into and across the edge of the wide valley, later descending – *with a view ahead of Llyn Gwynant* – then continuing down by a wall – *with Y Lliwedd towering above* – to cross a ladder-stile over it. A wide path now angles LEFT down the hillside to eventually join the wide stony Watkin Path below an old incline. Follow it down the hillside to go through a large gate and another ahead, then descend the path through woodland to the A498 at Pont Bethania. Turn RIGHT.

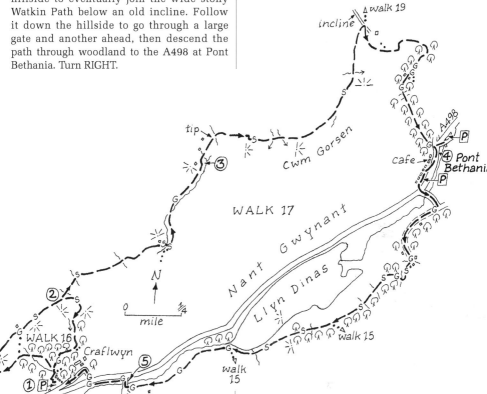

4 Go past houses to Gwynant café and on along the old road, then take the single track road opposite over the river. On the bend, go along the access track to Llyndy Isaf. Go past the house and outbuildings to a ladder-stile/gate. Follow the path round to a small gate and along the wood edge to a ladder-stile. The path continues along the edge of expansive tussocky reedy ground adjoining Llyn Dinas to a ladder-stile/gate then past woodland and a ladder-stile. After a stream the path rises to a ladder-stile, continues up through trees, then descends to a ladder-stile by Llyn Dinas. Continue along the path to a kissing gate at the end of the lake. Go past a large footbridge, and follow a path, initially near the river, to a road leading to Sygun Copper Mine.

5 Turn RIGHT to cross the bridge over the river to the A498. Go through a small gate on the left and follow the National Trust path over a footbridge and on by the river to a gate onto the A498. Cross to a nearby gate into Craflwyn. Go up the driveway, soon bending past the front of the hall, and continuing to the car park.

Nant Gwynant

WALK 18

HAFOD Y LLAN

DESCRIPTION A 2½ mile waymarked trail around Hafod y Llan Farm, featuring riverside and woodland walking. Hafod y Llan estate, with its 17thC farm, includes part of Snowdon and was purchased by public subscription in 1998. It is managed by the National Trust as a traditional organic farm. Allow about 1½ hours. A visit to nearby Gwynant cafe afterwards is recommended.
START Pont Bethania car park, Nant Gwynant SH 628507.
DIRECTIONS The car park lies on the A498 between Llyn Gwynant and Llyn Dinas, about 3 miles north-east of Beddgelert.

From the toilets follow the road over the river, then a path to the A498. Cross to the minor road opposite into Hafod y Llan estate. Go along the road, then take the signposted farm trail over a footbridge on the right and along the riverbank for ½ mile to cross a footbridge at a meeting of rivers. Turn LEFT, then RIGHT on the waymarked red arrow trail, through a wall gap, then along a field edge, initially by the river, to a gateway. Continue ahead along a stony track and through another gateway.

2 Just before a ladder-stile/gate follow the trail LEFT past a stone building and up near the wall. Go through a gap in the corner and turn LEFT along a path, soon bearing RIGHT and continuing between walls up to the large boundary wall of woodland. Turn LEFT and follow the trail between walls down to a small gate, then on beneath the woodland past small ruins. At the wall corner turn LEFT to cross a footbridge over the river. *Upstream is a power house for a new National Trust hydro electric scheme.* Keep ahead briefly then turn RIGHT to a gate into Hafod y Llan campsite. Go up the field edge to the wall end near the river to go through a gate beyond. Cross the stream and turn RIGHT up the field edge to a gate. Go up the stony path, initially above the river, to join the Watkin Path. Turn LEFT and follow the wide stony path down to a gate. Go

through another gate opposite and follow the Watkin Path past an information board and on through the wood down to the A498.

WALK 19

CWM LLAN

DESCRIPTION A 4 mile walk exploring an awe-inspiring enclosed upland valley beneath Snowdon. The route follows the delightful lower section of the Watkin Path to Snowdon through attractive woodland, then up past waterfalls into the dramatic setting of Cwm Llan containing famous Gladstone Rock, and the substantial remains of the former 19thC South Snowdon slate quarry, at just over 1000 ft/300 metres. It returns along an old tramway, descends back into the valley, later diverting to a delightful stone slab bridge by waterfalls. Allow about 2½ hours. An alternative 5 mile walk involves following the Hafod y Llan farm trail to join the Watkin Path higher up. A visit to nearby Gwynant cafe afterwards is recommended.
START As Walk 18.

The Watkin Path is named after Sir Edward Watkin, a Victorian railway tycoon and Liberal MP. who retired to the valley and who had the path constructed. The track, which was originally used by horse-drawn carriage as far as the old quarry, was open to the public in 1892 by the liberal Prime Minister William Gladstone, then 83. He addressed a crowd of over 2000 people at a huge boulder alongside the route, now known as Gladstone rock.

From the toilets follow the road over the river, then a path to the A498. Cross to the minor road opposite and take the signed Watkin Path from a small gate up through the wood to a small gate, and on past the site of Sir Edward Watkin's summer chalet and an information board to a large iron gate onto the original Watkin Path. Go through the gate ahead and follow the wide stony path as it winds its way up the hillside, later passing an old incline to gates into Yr Wyddfa National Nature Reserve. The path continues up above the Afon Cwm Llan and a series of

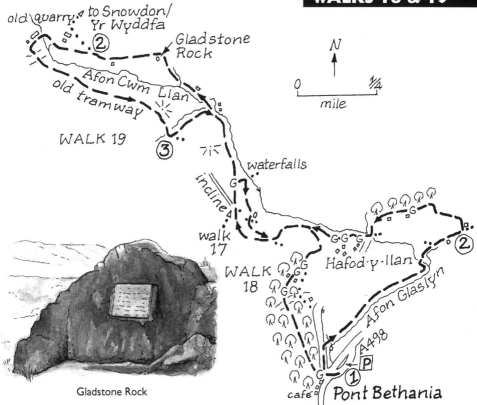

Gladstone Rock

Pont Bethania

small waterfalls. After passing the top falls by the former crushing mill for the Hafod-y-Llan copper mines high up on Y Lliwedd, the path levels out by a weir built for the National Trust's hydro-electric scheme. The wide path crosses the river and continues along Cwm Llan past slate fences, with the Snowdon ridge ahead. After passing the ruin of Plas Cwm Llan – *once the South Snowdon Slate Quarry manager's house* – the path continues up the valley past a small crag with a plaque - Gladstone rock – *with the old tramway visible on Yr Aran.*

2 About 120 yards before the remains of South Snowdon slate quarry ahead angle LEFT off the Watkin Path along a wide level green path. It passes beneath the buildings and waste tips to reach a lower part of the slate quarry. After crossing a bridge over the river go past the long ruined building, then the right hand side of a slate 'graveyard'.

Now bend along the old tramway and follow it along the slopes of Yr Aran. *The well constructed tramway carried slate from the quarry via inclines, to the road at Pont Bethania, from where it was taken by horse drawn cart to Porthmadog for loading onto ships.*

3 Later, take a substantial path back down into the valley – *high up on Y Lliwedd ahead are the remains of 17thC copper mines* – then return down the Watkin Path. After the gates, descend a path to a delightful stone slab bridge by waterfalls and pools – *a great place to linger.* Return a few yards then take a path on the left down through bracken and on by a wall to pass a ruin. At a crossroad of paths, keep ahead to the bottom of the old incline, then follow the former tramway to rejoin the Watkin Path. After the gate, either continue on the woodland path or go down the enclosed stony path, then along the minor road to the A498.

LLYN GWYNANT & CWM GLASLYN

DESCRIPTION A 5 mile figure of eight walk (**A**) combining a circuit of Llyn Gwynant with an exploration of an attractive enclosed valley beneath the Snowdon range, featuring the early 20th C Cwm-Dyli power station, or a 2¾ mile walk around Llyn Gwynant (**B**). Allow about 3½ and 2½ hours respectively
START Roadside parking near the northern end of Llyn Gwynant SH 648518.

1 Follow the roadside path north-east, then instructions in paragraph 3 of Walk 21 to the ladder-stile in the penultimate sentence. For **Walk A** now follow instructions in paragraph 2 below. (For **Walk B** continue to cross the stone slab footbridge, then follow instructions in paragraphs 4 of Walk 21 to the A498, then return on the pavement along the southern side of the lake.)

2 Cross the ladder-stile/sleeper bridge to a small gate. Go along the long field to cross a stile in its right-hand corner, a stream and a ladder-stile beyond. Follow the edge of the large reedy field to a stile onto a minor road. Follow it north along the valley, later passing Gwastadanas, to its end at a bridge over a fast flowing stream. (Here a small gate on the left provides a shorter option as shown.) Just beyond go down the left of two stony tracks – *with the Afon Glaslyn tumbling down the hillside ahead* – to the gated entrance of Cwm-Dyli power station by the river. Keep ahead. *This attractive utilitarian building (1906), linked by water pipes descending from Llyn Llydaw,* once provided local hillside quarries with power. A wooden shack was a mess hall and social centre for the workforce employed here.

3 At the end of the track go through a small gate ahead by a corrugated building, cross a stone slab bridge over the river and follow the fence round to cross a bridge over the pipeline and a ladder-stile. Follow the path to cross a facing ladder-stile, then through a long reedy field. Continue with a stonier path, flirting with the river, to eventually reach the stone slab bridge over the river, where you join Walk B to complete the circuit of Llyn Gwynant (see paragraph 1 above).

Llyn Gwynant

WALK 21

NANT GWYNANT
&
LLYN GWYNANT

DESCRIPTION A delightful 6¼ mile (**A**) or 4½ mile (**B**) walk, featuring woodland, upland pasture, and the beautiful Llyn Gwynant. Walk B returns along the lake's southern side. Walk A returns above its northern side. A visit to nearby Gwynant café afterwards is recommended. Allow about 4 and 3 hours respectively.
START Pont Bethania car park, Nant Gwynant SH 628507. See Walk 18.

I From the car park's northern end, take the signposted path along the driveway from Plas Gwynant lodge. Just past a cottage, follow the waymarked path up a stony track, then lane, passing above Plas Gwynant. At a cattle-grid, turn RIGHT down the waymarked path, over the river and on up to join a minor road. It rises steadily. After just over ½ mile, on the bend, go through a small gate on the left by a finger post. Follow the path to gates and on by the river to cross a footbridge over it. Follow the path across reedy ground, past a nearby house, through a wall gap and on across upland pasture – *enjoying good views of the Snowdon range* – to a small gate in a wall corner.

2 The initially boardwalked path continues through rhododendrons to a ladder-stile into Nant Gwynant. Follow the path through the forest, midway crossing a stream and ladder-stile. Eventually, at a wall corner, the path bends left briefly along the wood edge, then right to pass a stone barn. Ignore the cross-path and follow an improving path ahead across reedy ground, then down beside a wall. Just before a facing wall bear RIGHT along a faint green track, then go down an old walled stony track towards Llyn Gwynant. When it bends left, follow a path ahead down past the bend of a track, then down near a wall to join the stony track, which descends to the A498. Cross to the pavement opposite. (For **Walk B** turn left alongside the lake to rejoin the main route at point 5). Turn RIGHT and continue along the roadside path beside the lake.

3 After passing a ladder-stile/gate on the right, angle LEFT past an information board and on beside the lake to ladder-stile. Continue with the lakeside path, shortly rising across a gorse covered knoll, then descending to a small gate. Follow the path to a seat, then go along the shore. Where a piped stream enters the lake, turn RIGHT to reach a cross-track in Gwynant campsite. Go along another track ahead, through a gateway, past a side track, then keep ahead along the field edge to a ladder-stile. Turn LEFT to cross a delightful stone slab footbridge over the river.

4 Follow a path southwestwards near the river beneath the rock debris covered slope to a small gate and on beneath the steep slopes to a ladder-stile. The path now rises through a wood, past a viewpoint over the lake, then crosses the part wooded slope. After a stream, it bends left. Ignore a descending path, but follow a path up through the trees to a delightful crag overlooking the lake – *a good stopping place.* Continue through trees, soon taking the higher path up across a small rocky ridge. The path then descends through the trees and levels out. Take the right fork round the tree-topped knoll to a ladder-stile. The path continues up a part reedy valley, shortly levelling out before descending past old mine workings to a wall gap. After crossing a stream just beyond, turn LEFT towards a house. Turn RIGHT along its stony access track, shortly near the river. Just before a ladder-stile/gate by Ysgubor Bwlch, continue beside the river to cross an old stone slab footbridge over it to a gate into a field. Follow the path's right fork round to a ladder-stile and up to the A498.

5 Turn RIGHT and follow the pavement through the hamlet of Nantgwynant. Later take a signposted path up a narrow driveway on the left to Snowdon View. (Or continue along the pavement, then grass verge.) Go past the cottage and follow the path through the trees down to the lane near Plas Gwynant. Return along your outward route. *The nearby Gwynant café makes a rewarding end to the walk.*

WALK 22

MOEL EILIO

DESCRIPTION A 8 mile mountain walk featuring one of the finest grassy ridges in Snowdonia, offering extensive views of mountains, coast and Snowdon Mountain Railway. The route rises in stages above Llanberis, then climbs steadily to Moel Eilio (2381 ft/726 metres) and continues along the undulating ridge to Foel Goch. It then descends and returns along an attractive valley and near a river. Allow about 5½ hours. *For experienced hill walkers. Avoid in poor visibility*
START Snowdon Mountain Railway, Llanberis SH 584597.
DIRECTIONS The station is at the eastern end of the village.

The Snowdon Mountain Railway was built in 1896, with the 5 miles of track laid in just 72 working days. It works on a rack and pinion system, with the engines, some steam, pushing thousands of people to the summit each year.

I From the Snowdon Mountain Railway entrance follow the road towards the nearby Royal Victoria Hotel then turn RIGHT along Victoria Terrace. Shortly, take a road on the right across the river, under the railway bridge, past a children's play area and side road then turn LEFT across a cattle grid and follow the signposted footpath (waterfall) up a lane. Just past a cottage, go through a kissing gate on your left for a view of the waterfall. Continue up the lane past a track, then on the bend go through a kissing gate ahead. Go up the field edge to a waymarked path junction by a wall corner/kissing gate. Go across the wide path and on up to a kissing gate by a stream. Follow the stream up to another kissing gate then the wall up to a road by Hafod Uchaf. Go up the road to a gate onto a track.

2 Turn RIGHT to a ladder-stile/gate and follow the delightful bridleway to cross the Afon Goch and on to a minor road. Follow the road up past a ruin, then a green track up to a ladder-stile. The track rises

steadily across the hillside. *A new hydro-electric power scheme is being developed in former slate quarries north of the track.* Shortly after a gate, where the track levels out, take a wide path angling LEFT up beneath power cables. It continues up the hillside, shortly joining another stonier path for a climb up the northern slope of Moel Eilio, later alongside a fence to a ladder-stile, then another on the summit of Moel Eilio. Go to two small stone shelters ahead to enjoy great all-round views.

3 Return to the fence and follow it down to a ladder-stile – *with a view of Llyn Dwythwch below.* Continue down near the fence, soon joining a wide path which levels out, then rises to a ladder-stile. Now follow a faint path across the broad flat summit, soon descending and passing the end of a wall. The path now rises to pass above the head of Cwm Dwythwch, then goes along the small ridge of Foel Gron, before descending the broad steep grassy ridge. It then rises again up Foel Goch to a fence corner and continues alongside the fence to cross a ladder-stile ahead. Head half-RIGHT, then angle down the steep slope to a path junction at Bwlch Maesgwm. Bear LEFT on a stony path. It descends the western edge of Maesgwm valley, later levelling out to eventually accompany a wall to a gate. The path gently descends, later passing above ruins then a cottage. Go down its stony access track, through a gateway and on for a further 20 yards.

4 Go through a gate below, head down to a nearby ladder-stile. Follow the path across the reedy field to a stile, and on across the next to cross a bridge over the Afon Arddu. Turn LEFT up a boulder path then continue across upland pasture, descending to cross the railway line and on to a

Map labels

LLANBERIS
Snowdon
Mountain Railway
Hotel
waterfall
cafe
Afon Goch
Afon Hwch
WALK 23
Walk B
Afon Arddu
Llyn Dwythwch
WALK 22
N
0   ¼
mile
Foel Goch
Maesgwm
Bwlch Maesgwm

WALK 23

LLYN DWYTHWCH

DESCRIPTION A 3 mile walk (**A**) to the hidden mountain lake of Llyn Dwythwch (918 feet/280 metres) beneath Moel Eilio, and close views of Snowdon Mountain Railway. Allow about 2½ hours. A 2½ mile walk (**B**) excluding the lake is included.
START As Walk 22.

1 Follow instructions in paragraph **1** of **Walk 22**.

2 Follow the enclosed gated track LEFT down to a bridge over the Afon Hwch. Go up the track past a ladder-stile. (For **Walk B** continue south to point 4.) When it levels out go up a faint reedy green track on the right, then continue towards Moel Eilio. Shortly, angle RIGHT to join the fence above the river, soon bending south on an improving path to reach Llyn Dwythwch. Bear LEFT along the end of the lake, then go up a path angling LEFT. Continue past piles of stones to the bottom of the heather slope ahead. Here follow a good path LEFT, soon bending across the mid-slopes, then descending to rejoin the track by ruins. Follow it RIGHT for about 200 yards, then follow instructions in paragraph 4 of Walk 22.

road. Follow it down past Pen y Cuenant Isaf café back to the start.

Llyn Dwythwch

WALK 24
LLYN OGWEN

DESCRIPTION A 3 mile low-level walk around Llyn Ogwen, one of the shallowest lakes in Snowdonia enclosed by mountains, featuring delightful Ogwen waterfall and a new Visitor Centre and cafe at its western end. Its follows a roadside pavement along its southern side and a waymarked National Trust path, rocky and wet in places, along its northern side, offering great lake and mountain views without the crowds. Allow about 2¼ hours

START Car park on the A5 by Llyn Ogwen SH 656602.

DIRECTIONS Travelling west along the A5 from Capel Curig, when you reach Llyn Ogwen, park in the third National Trust Glyderau car park on the left – the last before Ogwen Cottage.

1 Follow the pavement opposite east above Llyn Ogwen – *with Tryfan towering above*. Go past the end of the lake then turn LEFT on a signposted path along a track over the river, then past Glan Dena into Open Access land. Continue along the stony track. Just before a gate at the farm entrance, take the waymarked National Trust path on the right up to cross a ladder-stile in the wall. At a waymark post just beyond a nearby stream, ignore the rising red stony path and take another path on the left down through bracken and reeds to another post. Follow the waymarked path above the farm, then down to cross two forks of the Afon Lloer and a stile. Continue with the path, guided by regular white-topped posts across the reedy, stone covered terrain – *with great views of Llyn Ogwen,Tryfan, Y Garn, and Pen-yr Ole Wen up to your right* – to another stile.

2 After about 100 yards, the path splits. Keep with the lower waymarked left fork, over a stream, across a rock slab, and on past further posts, passing under electricity cables, then following them across the hillside. The path passes through a wall gap, then under the cables and heads towards Llyn Ogwen, continuing down to a ladder-

stile near the lake. The path soon passes an old pill box and continues beside the lake to its end, then passes through an area of large boulders to join the river, then reach the A5. *Note the remains of an old arched stone bridge beneath the road bridge.* First go through a small gate opposite to a crag overlooking Rhaeadr Ogwen, then follow the pavement up to a side road just before Ogwen Cottage Outdoor Centre. Follow it to the nearby Visitor Centre and café. Return to follow the pavement alongside the lake back to the start.

WALK 25
LLYN IDWAL

DESCRIPTION A 3¼ mile walk (**A**) combining a short section alongside Llyn Ogwen with a circuit of Llyn Idwal, lying at about 1200 ft/365 metres within the dramatic glacial valley of Cwm Idwal – the first National Nature Reserve in Wales – whose rock faces support important rare plants. Allow about 2½ hours. Included is a 3 mile (**B**) walk with a more direct finish across open ground and a shorter 2 mile walk (**C**). Walks A/C can be shortened by starting from the Snowdonia National Park pay & display car park near the Visitor Centre at SH 649604.

START As Walk 24.

1 Follow the pavement west alongside the lake, then take the side road by Ogwen Cottage Outdoor Centre to the nearby Visitor Centre, café and toilets. Go up the wide stony path past the near end of the Centre. After a few yards turn RIGHT up a side path between rock faces to a ladder-stile. Follow the path up through the gully, soon climbing out of its right side to a stile. The path continues across open ground, soon rising steadily – *with views of Tryfan, the Glyders and Cwm Idwal/Y Garn ahead* – then crosses level ground to a stile in a fence – *with a view of Llyn Idwal.* Follow the path ahead and after about 50 yards, when it bends right up towards Y Garn, follow another path ahead down towards the lake, over a cross-path, to reach the stony shore. (For **Walk C** turn left alongside the lake, then follow a path to a footbridge over the lake's outlet to

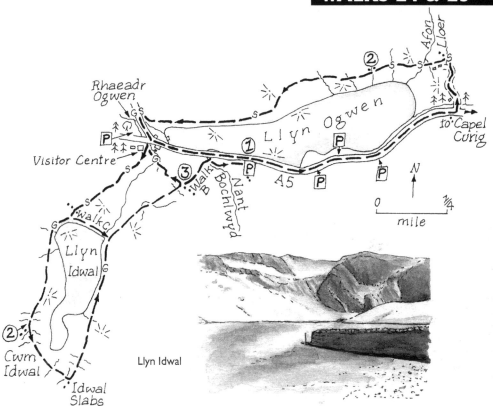

Llyn Idwal

join the return path beyond.) Turn RIGHT along the shore to a gate in the wall and follow the path alongside the lake, soon rising and continuing towards the head of the valley.

2 Later, just before the main path begins to rise towards Twll Ddu (Devil's Kitchen) ahead – *a narrow cleft in the mountain* – take a stony path on the left down to cross two streams. Continue across level ground beyond the end of the lake towards Idwal Slabs – *a famous rock climbing site* – then follow a meandering stone path up to join a cross-path beneath the Slabs. Follow it LEFT back along the eastern side of Cwm Idwal, past the lake and through a gate. After passing the footbridge over the lake's outlet, continue with the wide stony path, shortly descending – *with a view of Llyn Ogwen ahead.*

3 Just after it bends left you have a choice. For **Walk A** continue down the main path to a footbridge over the river and on down to join your outward route near the Visitor Centre. (For **Walk B**, take a stony path on the right. After a few yards, turn left along a green path down towards Llyn Ogwen. When it splits, follow the path left down the hillside, then descend past a wettish area to a ladder-stile by the road (an alternative return option). Cross the bridge over the river. Go past another ladder-stile and National Trust sign. Follow a path onto the small ridge, then up towards Tryfan, parallel with the nearby river. After about 80 yards, at the sharp end of a rocky ridge, turn left along another path down to the fence overlooking the road, then the wall to a ladder-stile into the car park.)

WALK 26

MOEL FABAN, LLEFN & GYRN

DESCRIPTION A 5½ mile walk (**A**), generally on good paths, exploring the attractive upland landscape near Bethesda, featuring three outlying foothills of the Carneddau range, offering extensive coastal and mountain views. The route rises from Bethesda into Open Access land, then climbs up and across Moel Faban (1342 ft/409 metres) before gently descending to a point overlooking the narrow pass of Bwlch ym Mhwll-le. From its eastern end the route makes a short climb onto the grassy top of nearby Llefn (1453 ft/443 metres), then continues up to the summit of Gyrn (1778 ft/542 metres). The walk returns through Bwlch ym Mhwll-le or via its northern rim (route b), then the lower western slope of Moel Faban. Allow about 3½ hours. Avoid in poor visibility. A less demanding but equally enjoyable 3 mile walk (**B**) omitting Llefn and Gyrn is included.

START Top car park, Bethesda [SH 624668].

DIRECTIONS In the centre of Bethesda take the road signposted to the Police station, library and car park. A road on the right leads to the car park.

B *ethesda became an important slate quarrying community as nearby Penrhyn Quarry grew into the largest slate quarry in the world at the end of the 19thC, employing 3,000 men.*

I From the north eastern corner of the car park join a stony access track. Follow it up past a small stone building, then take a path's right fork up through trees to a road. Turn RIGHT past the side road of Bryn Teg and continue along the road (Stryd Cefnfaes) to crossroads. Go to the no through road opposite (Ffordd Ffrydlas), then immediately turn LEFT up an initially stepped enclosed surfaced path to a road above. Turn RIGHT then LEFT up Cilfodan. Follow it up into open country to its end by Tanyfoel terraced cottages. Continue ahead on a signposted path up an initially walled access track, then when it bends towards a house continue

ahead up a delightful part walled path to a kissing gate into Open Access land.

2 Go straight up the slope ahead, over a stream, and follow a clear path up the gorse covered southern slope of Moel Faban, then across its stone covered summit featuring two large stone shelters. *There are great views to Bangor, Penrhyn Castle, Menai Strait, Traeth Lafan and Anglesey beyond, and a panorama of mountains inland. Ahead is Llefn and the shapely peak of Gyrn.* The path now descends to a cross-path overlooking the narrow pass of Bwlch ym Mhwll-le. (For **Walk B** follow the improving path left down to join a wide path at point 4.) Follow it RIGHT down to cross a reedy area at the end of the bwlch. Now head up towards Llefn, soon crossing a wide cross-path. Continue across the gorse and stone covered ground, soon climbing more steeply to the left of scree to

follow a good path across Llefn's grassy summit – *soon with a reservoir visible down to the left.* The path now heads towards Gyrn, goes over a cross-path, then begins to rise, soon more steeply, to briefly join a wider path. Head across the left shoulder of the nearby rocky summit, then turn RIGHT up onto the final top with its small stone shelter – *with new views into a wild upland landscape overlooked by Moel Wnion ahead and the nearby mountain tops of Drosgl, Bera Mawr & Bera Bach.*

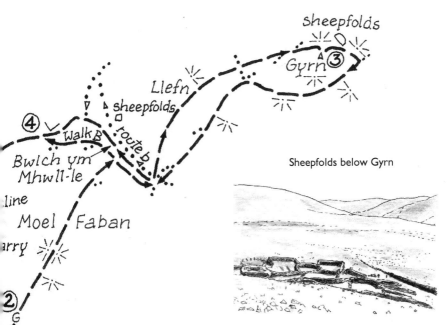

sheepfolds

Gyrn ③

Llefn
sheepfolds

④
Walk B route b
Bwlch ym
Mhwll-le

line
Moel Faban

arry

②
G

Sheepfolds below Gyrn

3 Descend north east to overlook a complex of sheepfolds, then work your way down the stone covered slope to their right hand end. Continue south east down the slope for about 50 yards, then turn RIGHT along a narrow cross-path. The improving path heads south-west then west down beneath Gyrn, passing a small quarry. At a crossroad of paths take the wide path half-LEFT (south-west) to pass beneath the eastern slopes of Llefn. Continue down the path's wider left fork and past another path angling right. At a cross-path keep ahead, bending RIGHT to the reedy area at the end of Bwlch ym Mhwll-le. (For the alternative **Route B** follow the cross-path right along the northern rim of the bwlch, then down beneath large sheepfolds to join a wide path at a wall corner. Follow it left down to the bottom of the bwlch and on to point 4.) Follow a path along the left hand side of the narrow pass, soon descending through it to join the bend of a wide path. Follow it LEFT to pass a fence corner.

4 Continue with the delightful wide path across the lower gorse covered western slopes of Moel Faban. After briefly joining a wall continue with the wide path (an old tramway) across the hillside, over an old incline, past a quarry and across an area of waste. As it begins to rise, angle RIGHT down past a large 'wall' of slate waste, then just before a boundary wall turn RIGHT down past the perimeter fence of a covered reservoir. Follow the fence round to a kissing gate. Follow the main path down through gorse and small trees, across quarry waste to another kissing gate, then down to a kissing gate/gate by a house. Go down its access lane to a road. Follow it LEFT past houses. At a junction by Y Sior pub, turn RIGHT past a slate sculpture at a viewing area, and down a stepped walled path to a road. Follow the pavement opposite LEFT down past a children's play area. At the bottom junction by terraced houses turn RIGHT down to go through a large kissing gate. Follow a stony path LEFT down through an open area of small trees to the car park.

WALK 27
COEDYDD ABER

DESCRIPTION A 5¾ mile (**A**) walk through the Coedydd Aber National Nature Reserve, featuring the stunning Aber Falls (Rhaedr Fawr) in its magnificent mountain setting. The route takes the popular trail to Aber Falls, then passes another waterfall, before making a steady ascent across open slopes. It then follows a highly scenic upland section of the North Wales Path, offering extensive coastal views, before descending a side valley and following field paths to Abergwyngregyn. Allow about 3½ hours. The route includes a shorter 3¾ mile (**B**) walk and a simple 2½ mile circuit (**C**) to Aber Falls.

START Bont Newydd, Abergwyngregyn [SH 662720]

DIRECTIONS Turn off the A55 signposted to Abergwyngregyn, and follow the road south through the village and along the wooded valley to reach a parking area just before the road crosses the river (Bont Newydd). An alternative Aber Forestry Commission car park/toilets is signposted from the other side of the bridge. Both car parks are pay and display. (From the forestry car park return down the road, then take the signposted path to Aber Falls to cross a footbridge over the river, and up through the trees. Go along the forestry track ahead to gates. Follow the green track down to join the stony track by an information board.) An alternative start can be made from the free village car park.

*C*oedydd Aber, *managed by the Countryside Council for Wales, is located in a steep-sided valley between the Carneddau mountains and the coastal plain. Extensive archaeological remains, including prehistoric burial and settlement sites, reveal man's association with this sheltered valley and surrounding uplands for over 3000 years. Its dense mixed woodland is now the home of both woodland and mountain birds. The famous waterfall, formed during the Ice Age, has attracted visitors since the late 18thC, aided by the opening* of the post road in the 1820s and the railway in 1848. The river rises as Yr Afon Goch (red river) and flows over the 100 foot rock face to become Afon Rhaedr Fawr (the river of the great falls) which flows down to the sea. It is one of the steepest rivers from source to mouth in England and Wales.

Go through the kissing gate at the end of Bont Newydd (the new bridge) built in the 1820s to enter Coedydd Aber. Follow the path alongside the river. After crossing a footbridge over the river, go through a small gate, then turn RIGHT up a stony track. Keep with the main track signposted to the waterfall, as it climbs steadily up the increasingly open wooded valley, soon giving views to the mountains ahead, to reach Nant Rhaedr Visitor Centre. *This was originally a Welsh tyddyn (smallholding), which once sold tea and home-made lemonade to Victorian visitors on route to the Falls, and now contains an exhibition.* Continue along the wide stony path and suddenly, the impressive waterfall comes into view. The path now narrows and continues up to a small gate and on to reach the base of the waterfall. (Retrace your steps then for **Walk C**, return to the gate, cross the nearby ladder-stile, and follow the waymarked path angling up the rocky slope to a ladder-stile into the forest. Follow the path through the forest, then alongside its boundary to rejoin your outward route.)

2 For **Walk A**, cross the footbridge over the river. Follow the path up above the river to a close viewpoint of the waterfall, then go to a nearby gate and follow the waymarked North Wales Path, soon alongside a wall beneath impressive crags. After passing a ladder-stile the path descends to a footbridge over a river beneath another waterfall. The path now continues over several streams, later bending north and rising steadily up the part bracken covered slope and on across the hillside to reach a ladder-stile/gate. Continue up a green track, past a seat – *a good stopping place* – to another ladder-stile. The track continues up to a further ladder-stile, then passes beneath power cables. Shortly the track makes a gen-

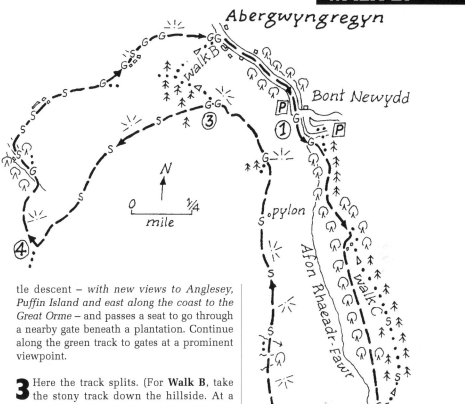

Abergwyngregyn

Bont Newydd

Afon Rhaeadr-Fawr

pylon

Falls

Rhaeadr Fawr
Aber Falls

N

0   ¼
mile

tle descent – *with new views to Anglesey, Puffin Island and east along the coast to the Great Orme* – and passes a seat to go through a nearby gate beneath a plantation. Continue along the green track to gates at a prominent viewpoint.

3 Here the track splits. (For **Walk B**, take the stony track down the hillside. At a waymark post turn right, and follow a path angling down the steep slope to reach the road.) Follow the level green track on the waymarked NWP through gates ahead, then across the hillside to a kissing gate. Continue ahead alongside the fence – *enjoying panoramic coastal views* – to a ladder-stile. Keep ahead. After another ladder-stile follow the faint green track passing above a steep side valley. Just before the next ladder-stile bend RIGHT with the track.

4 Follow the improving track down the hillside towards the coast into the side valley, over a stream and through a gate into a field. Leave the track and go down the left field edge to a ladder-stile near a cottage. Go down its access track, then after about 30 yards, at a waymark post in the roots of a large tree, turn RIGHT up the bank. Go across the field, over a ladder-stile ahead, and on across the next field to another ladder-stile. Continue by trees above farm buildings, then

angle down through the trees to a gate at the end of outbuildings. Go ahead between the house and an outbuilding through gates into a field. Go ahead across the field to a ladder-stile/gate by attractive slate fencing. Continue ahead along a faint track to a kissing gate/gate by a descending track. Go down the green track to a kissing gate by a cottage, and on over a ladder-stile ahead. Go across the field to a kissing gate, then along the next field edge to another kissing gate.

5 Follow the path across the bracken-covered slope overlooking Abergwyngregyn, past a seat, after which it gently descends. When it splits continue on the upper right fork between fences to a gate and on down to the road. Follow it back to the start.

WALK 29

GARREG FAWR

DESCRIPTION A 3¼ mile (**A**) or 3 mile (**B**) walk using the network of delightful green paths and tracks to explore the small hill of Garreg Fawr (1194 feet/ 364 metres), now an Open Access area, offering panoramic views. Walk A visits its craggy top, then returns with Walk B down the North Wales Path (NWP). Allow about 2–2½ hours.

START Valley Road, Llanfairfechan
[SH 688742]

DIRECTIONS Turn off the A55 into Llanfairfechan. At traffic lights turn up Village Road, passing the school and shops. At a junction, turn left up Bryn Road, soon becoming Valley Road to find a large parking area on the right by a side road at the last houses.

I Follow the side road across a bridge over the river, then turn LEFT between garages and go up a stepped path to a road above. Follow it west past Bron Cae cottages then take a signposted path up the driveway to Tanrallt Ucha. On the bend follow a waymarked enclosed path to a kissing gate, then behind the farm. Just before a fence corner turn RIGHT and follow a wide green path up the gorse/bracken covered hillside to a path junction. Turn RIGHT and follow another delightful path up to a kissing gate. Turn LEFT and follow the wall up the gorse covered hillside towards the craggy top of Garreg Fawr. At the top wall corner continue along a level narrow green track above the wall, soon rising steadily then heading south and levelling out – *offering a panorama of mountains.* Continue with the green track's right fork across the eastern slopes of Garreg Fawr to eventually reach a junction of tracks at a NWP waymark post.

2 Turn sharp RIGHT and follow the North Wales Path north. At the next waymark post the track splits. (For **Walk B** continue with the NWP down its left fork.) For **Walk A** take the right fork and follow the meandering green track across the wide flattish top of Garreg Fawr to reach its craggy

top. Keep ahead down the slope towards Llanfairfechan, passing a fence protecting a sharp drop, then descend to a wide green cross-path. Follow it LEFT. After about 45 yards turn LEFT past stone post no. 8 and continue below stone sheepfolds and Garreg Fawr's western slopes. At another stone post, descend to a nearby wooden waymark post to rejoin the North Wales Path. Follow it down through gorse, past side paths, stone post no. 9 and a nearby old settlement site, to the kissing gate. Go down your outward route past the seat, then keep ahead down to a ladder-stile. Follow the enclosed path down to another ladder-stile, then go across a field to a road. Follow it LEFT back to your outward stepped path.

WALK 28

ROMAN ROAD

DESCRIPTION A 6 mile walk featuring attractive upland pasture, delightful green tracks on Garreg Fawr, a section of a former Roman Road, which it joins at a height of 1279 feet, and extensive views. Allow about 4 hours. The walk can be accessed from Bont Newydd, Abergwyngregyn or a small road end car park as shown.

START Valley Road, Llanfairfechan
[SH 688742]

DIRECTIONS See **Walk 29**.

B eneath the foot-hills of the north-ern Carneddau is a prehistoric mountain trackway which became part of a Roman road which ran from Canovium fort in the Conwy Valley to Segontium in Caernarfon. Later it became an important drovers route, with Aber serving as a stopping station. Traditionally, these upland pastures were grazed by cattle during the summer, but by the early 19thC, sheep had taken over. Wild ponies still graze here.

Abergwyngreg
Bont Newydd

I Follow the side road across a bridge over the river, then turn LEFT between garages and go up a stepped path to a road above. Follow the road (Terrace Walk) west past

Bron Cae cottages. After ⅓ mile the road bends left. At a house, go through a bridle-gate and follow the enclosed rock based track up to a kissing gate/gate. Continue with the green track, soon rising away from the wall up the gorse covered hillside. It then follows another wall up into open country, later joining the waymarked North Wales Path. This delightful narrow green track rises across the slopes of Garreg Fawr, then continues to a junction of tracks at a waymark post near a wall corner.

3 Before power cables, cross a stone stile on the right. Follow the path up the bracken covered slope ahead to a level path just to the left of the large pylon base. Here angle LEFT up to join a higher cross path leading from the top pylon foot. Follow it across the steep gorse covered hillside – *soon with a view to Anglesey*. The path rises gently to cross exposed rocks then contours across less steep terrain and passes through bracken towards the large wall ahead. Take its less distinct right fork to pass just to the right of a solitary tree ahead. Now angle RIGHT up a path, soon joining another. Just before the wall turn RIGHT up to a ladder-stile. Continue ahead beside the wall down two fields.

4 After crossing an iron ladder-stile go slightly RIGHT down the large field to join the distant wall ahead. Follow it down to cross a ladder-stile in the corner onto a green track below. Follow a path opposite down through trees to stepping stones over the river, then up to a kissing gate. Go half-LEFT across the field to a ladder-stile/gate, then go down the lane. On the bend take a signposted path on the right to a kissing gate. Follow the fence down and round beneath the bracken/gorse-covered hillside to a gate by a house. Go along a green track, through another gate then follow Llys-y-Gwynt farm's access track ahead to join a road. Shortly, turn RIGHT up Terrace Walk, soon joining your outward route.

Llanfairfechan

N

0 ¼ mile

sheepfolds

Garreg Fawr

Walk 28

Walk 29

Walk 29A

WALK 28

Foel Ganol

2 Follow the stony track ahead up to a large pylon. Take the track's right fork up past another pylon to a stony track – *the Roman Road*. Turn RIGHT and follow the track on a steady descent in stages westwards towards Aber. After 1 mile the track bends south beside a large wall, soon descending then bending down to a gate. Go along the narrow walled road, soon descending.

DRUIDS CIRCLE & FOEL LUS

DESCRIPTION A 5¼ mile (**A**) or 4¼ mile (**B**) walk exploring the attractive hills and upland plateau above Penmaenmawr, featuring the famous Bronze Age Druids Circle, other ancient groups of stones, and superb views. **Walk A** includes an exhilarating high level panoramic walk around Foel Lus created to celebrate Queen Victoria's Jubilee in 1887. There is also an option to climb to the top of Foel Lus (1188 feet/362 metres). After the initial steep ascent to reach the Circle standing at just over 1300 feet/400 metres, the rest of the route offers delightful walking. Allow about 3½ hours.

START Car park by the library, Penmaenmawr [SH 719763].

DIRECTIONS At crossroads in the centre of Penmaenmawr go up Fernbrook road, signposted to the library to find a large car park on the right. This walk is also accessible by bus or train.

The hills and upland plateau above *Penmaenmawr are rich in archaeological evidence of early man. On the hill that towers above the town to the south, heavily scarred by quarrying for granite, which continues to this day, is the site of Graiglwyd Neolithic axe factory – the third largest production centre in Britain. Stone stronger than flint was first removed in blocks, then pieces flaked by hammerstone into rough shape, before being polished and attached to wooden handles. As Neolithic man began to settle on the land, axes were needed for clearing dense forest to create pasture, and building wooden houses. Axes made here have been found throughout Britain, indicating the existence of an extensive trading network. Later, partly encouraged by an improvement in climate, early Bronze Age man moved into the uplands, leaving behind an extensive range of burial and ritual monuments.*

I From the car park, turn RIGHT up the road and just past Y Berllan, go up a railed stepped pathway on the right. At its top turn RIGHT along a lane past houses, and at a road junction, turn LEFT. After a few yards, bear RIGHT on a tarmaced path past the end of Llys Machno up to a road. Go up the road to a kissing gate ahead. Go up the tree-lined path to a gate by a ruin and on up a field to a kissing-gate onto a road. Follow it LEFT, then turn RIGHT up a driveway on a signposted path. Follow the waymarked path to the left of buildings, past a corner wall and up to a kissing gate. Now follow the delightful green path up the hillside, soon near a fence past a small wood. At the fence corner keep with the main path rising steadily up the edge of an attractive side valley. A bench seat and excellent views looking back assist in the increasingly steep climb. *Nearby to the west is the heavily quarried Graiglwyd mountain and site of the Neolithic axe factory.* After another bench seat the path crosses a low concrete footbridge across a stream and a reedy area, then rises to a kissing gate in the wall ahead. Go up the slope ahead to join the North Wales Path at a waymark post. Turn RIGHT and follow the path west near the wall to reach a narrow track by a waymark post.

2 Here, turn LEFT along the green track – *past the scant remains of a stone circle* – which quickly becomes a path. Keep to its higher right fork to unexpectedly reach a more substantial stone circle on the edge of a plateau leading to Tal y Fan and grazed by wild ponies. A little further on is the Druids Circle – *an impressive large embanked stone circle dating from the 2nd millennium BC which, in the 18thC was often sketched by travellers who passed by on the ancient mountain road below. It was probably originally used for rituals, then later for burials, as evidenced by the cremated remains of several young children found in its centre.* Descend across a gully and follow the clear path down and along to join the NWP/WCP at a waymark post. Just to your right is the remains of another small stone circle.

3 Continue with the NWP/WCP, soon near a wall – *enjoying extensive coastal views from Llandudno to Rhyl.* After going through a kissing gate in the wall the path descends then bears LEFT along a tree-lined green

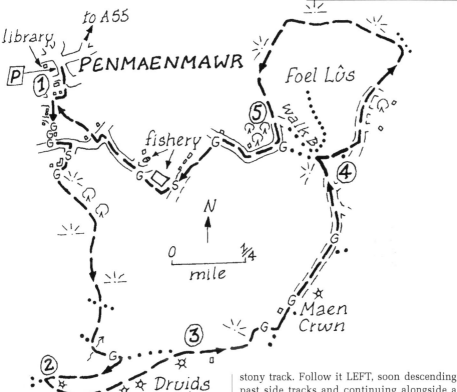

to A55

library

PENMAENMAWR

Foel Lûs

walk B

fishery

N

0   ¼
mile

Druids circle

Maen Crwn

track to pass Bryn Derwydd. *Nearby is Maen Crwn, a large glacial erratic stone.* After a gate continue along the track. *In the field to your right are several small stones – the remains of a stone circle.* When the North Wales Path goes through a gate on the right, continue along the track to a kissing gate/gate and on to join another track coming in from the right. Keep ahead.

4 Go past another track on the right (another option – you join it shortly), then a seat and a stone route marker, after which the track descends – *offering dramatic views over Penmaenmawr and across to Anglesey.* (For **Walk B** either descend the steep slope on the left to a kissing gate or continue down the track to point **5**.) Just beyond the bend where the track levels out take a path angling back on the right up the heather slope. Keep to its right fork (the left fork offers an optional climb to the top of Foel Lus) to join the

stony track. Follow it LEFT, soon descending past side tracks and continuing alongside a wall. At the wall corner, when the track bends down to a house, continue straight ahead on a path through heather, soon descending past telegraph poles – *with a superb view towards the Great Orme, Conwy Mountain, and Sychnant Pass.* At a junction of paths, bear LEFT past a seat to follow the higher Jubilee Path contouring around the steep slopes of Foel Lus – *enjoying breathtaking coastal views.*

5 After passing through the 'gateway' to the Jubilee Path – go down the road. Later, go through a kissing gate on the left opposite an underground reservoir. Go along the field edge passing above a farm, later joining its access track, then cross a ladder-stile on the right. Follow the fenced path round the edge of the fishery and past the caravan site to a kissing gate, then continue down a lane. At a road junction, turn LEFT, and after a few yards RIGHT to follow an enclosed path to join your outward route by Llys Machno.

PRONUNCIATION

Welsh	English equivalent
c	always hard, as in **c**at
ch	as in the Scottish word lo**ch**
dd	as th in **th**en
f	as f in o**f**
ff	as ff in o**ff**
g	always hard as in **g**ot
ll	no real equivalent. It is like 'th' in then, but with an 'L' sound added to it, giving 'thlan' for the pronunciation of the Welsh 'Llan'.

In Welsh the accent usually falls on the last-but-one syllable of a word.

KEY TO THE MAPS

- ➡ Walk route and direction
- ═ Metalled road
- --- Unsurfaced road
- •••• Footpath/route adjoining walk route
- ~~→ River/stream
- ⚘ 🌳 Trees
- ▬■▬ Railway
- **G** Gate
- **S** Stile
- F.B. Footbridge
- ☼ Viewpoint
- P Parking
- T Telephone

THE COUNTRYSIDE CODE

- Be safe – plan ahead and follow any signs
- Leave gates and property as you find them
- Protect plants and animals, and take your litter home
- Keep dogs under close control
- Consider other people

Open Access
Some routes cross areas of land where walkers have the legal right of access under The CRoW Act 2000 introduced in May 2005. Access can be subject to restrictions and closure for land management or safety reasons for up to 28 days a year. Details from: www.naturalresourceswales.gov.uk. Please respect any notices.

About the author, David Berry

David is an experienced walker with a love of the countryside and an interest in local history. He is the author of a series of walks guidebooks covering North Wales, where he has lived and worked for many years, and been a freelance writer for Walking Wales magazine. He has also worked as a Rights of Way surveyor across North Wales and served as a member of Denbighshire Local Access Forum. For more information visit: www.davidberrywalks.co.uk

Published by **Kittiwake-Books Limited**
3 Glantwymyn Village Workshops, Glantwymyn, Machynlleth, Montgomeryshire SY20 8LY

© Text & map research: David Berry 2015
© Maps & illustrations: Kittiwake-Books Ltd 2015
Drawings by Morag Perrott
Cover photos: Main: Grib Ddu, Walk 15. *Inset:* St Celynin's Church, Walk 5. *David Berry.*

Care has been taken to be accurate. However neither the author nor the publisher can accept responsibility for any errors which may appear, or their consequences. If you are in any doubt about access, check before you proceed.

Printed by Zenith Media, Pontypool.

ISBN: **978 1 908748 25 6**